GAME CHANGER: SK-11

A YOUNG ATHLETE'S SUCCESS, A PARENT'S GRIEF

By

RICHARD KENDRICK

WRITE SERVICES PRESS

Published by:

Write Services Press, Horn Lake, MS 38637
Writeservicespress.com

© **2021 Richard M. Kendrick**

Gamechangersk11@yahoo.com
https://sk11livelovedream.com

Design:

Interior: Write Services Press

Graphics © Richard M. Kendrick

Disclaimer:

The events related in this book are accurate to the best of the author's memory and available public records. The views, thoughts, and opinions expressed in the text belong solely to the author, and not necessarily to the author's employer, organization, committee, or other group or individual except as expressly identified.

Hardcover ISBN-13: 978-1-954373-06-8
Paperback ISBN-13: 978-1-954373-05-1
Digital ISBN-13: 978-1-954373-07-5

Library of Congress Control Number: 2021943641

Printed in USA

DEDICATION

To My Son

Growing up, I always felt semi-lost and scared. When you came, I gained a sense of something bigger and stronger. It was like my sails caught the wind. Suddenly, this ship with no direction was given its true bearing, pointed toward what it was meant for, and it was full speed ahead. From the moment you came, my purpose, drive, and sense of reason became clear. The 27-year-old boy I was became someone with a purpose.

I finally had someone that would always love me and never leave me regardless of my wrong doings. Its why this pain is even deeper than most losses, and something I believe is a trueness to all parents. We all know there is this little person that will always be there for us. As we gaze into your infant faces, we realize we will never be fully alone again. I had a son, and love for the rest of my life for the first time in my life, and I cherished it beyond anything I'd ever imagined.

I wrote this book to tell everyone about how you changed me and how a child can truly give one a purpose when there is no direction. I was a flawed father. I made many mistakes, but one thing I always made certain of was to let you and your sister know just how much you meant to me and how much I love you and always will, forever. This love is the strongest I've ever experienced.

The pain, grief as they call it, makes everything else in life seem so small and petty. The things that used to hurt, bother, or upset me before truly mean nothing now. Your Dad's feelings still get hurt, and some emotions still exist. But the lingering effects are not really there anymore. I'm sorry for the way you saw me as now I know those heartaches and pains that used to consume me are nothing.

I'm sorry you saw me so weak. I wish I could have been stronger for you in so many ways. But I do know deep in my heart, mind, body, and soul, you knew how much I loved you. And you know I'm coming to you soon, the blink of an eye in God's eyes. We will be together again ...

I miss you Stevo.

Love Dad

CONTENTS

INTRODUCTION

Ode to Stevo

Younger players in the wings, in the dugouts, in the stands when you are playing watch that big hitter—you, Stevo. They inhale, hold their breath for a single, magical moment—until your bat smacks that ball deep into whichever field—right, left, center—way out there. In their minds, they see that baseball flying like a shooting star. The sky was the limit for a player like you. Nothing could stop you. You had it all—the talent, the background, the training, the character. The fans were already lining up to wonder at your potential.

They loved you not only because of your clear mastery of the game, but because of your stellar spirit. Off the field, you were kind and generous, giving your gifts freely to everyone around you, constantly working to help elevate others no matter their age or ability. When you smacked that ball out of the park, spectators saw you lifting everyone in the park with you.

1

These are the moments etched into those kids' minds, moments that are eternal even as they pass. These are moments they dream of, when one day they might hit that fast pitch and hear the fans, teammates, and coaches celebrate. These are the moments that inspire them. That is what you did. This is what you left to this community, for your teammates, and with your family.

CHAPTER 1: PLAYER DOWN

It was somewhere I never once imagined I'd be, standing there in the front of a church watching streams of people coming from all sides to pay their last respects to my beautiful boy. It's a day every parent fears, yet there I was, living the nightmare. It was surreal. It's still hard to wrap my head around the emotions of that day. I stood there consumed by grief on the saddest day of my life while, at the same time, feeling the pride and joy of realizing what a wonderful son I'd raised. That joy would lead down another deep spiral of despair that he was lost to us, and so the cycle went.

The church wasn't small, and my boy wasn't old, just a few weeks shy of his 20th birthday, but we had to open up both side doors to handle the numbers of people who came. We also had to extend our planned-for three hours of visitation to five. In such a short lifetime, he'd already made such a tremendous impact. Family and close friends came toward me up the center aisle while friends, teammates, and coaches from high school approached from the right and a similar group from college approached from the left. Maybe I shouldn't have been, but I was a little surprised by how many people from his college came. He'd only attended one full semester by then, though he had already led all hitters and was well on his way toward securing his starting spot at first base during the fall baseball season.

A lot of thought went into the church decorations for the event. Steven Kendrick, my son Stevo, was always an athlete, hunter, and fisher. It seemed natural to decorate his casket like a duck blind. Maybe it made it a little easier, too, to think of him simply off on another hunting trip. The duck decoys used within the flower arrangements made it feel more normal somehow, even though there wasn't anything normal about this at all.

My son rested, fully decked out in my best Drake hunting shirt like he just couldn't wait to get on with the hunt. He was even wearing sunglasses and a hat, both necessary because of the damage from the accident that killed him, but he looked like my son. The sunglasses had come from my truck.

The first time I saw my son after the accident, it was unbearable to look at his brokenness. I had the funeral director retrieve the glasses from my truck for me and I placed them on his face myself. As soon as the glasses were in place, the injuries were covered enough to see my son's face again. It gave me some peace to look at him without feeling the visceral pain. Everyone commented on how peaceful he looked, how much he looked just like the same Stevo they knew.

Many of the details of that day are hazy. The rest are difficult, if not impossible, to think about much less talk or write about. It's a day you don't expect to see as a parent. I remember thinking about how appropriate the song choices had been, how much thought had gone into every detail. Had I been involved in any of that?

The night before the funeral, I'd felt so lost. The only thing I could think of to do was pack Stevo's hunting backpack. I packed all his favorite snacks and drinks, just like we would before heading out on any of our adventures. I made doubly sure he had everything. Flashlight, batteries, extra change of clothes, shaving razor, soap, deodorant, blanket. I made a complete list and placed the list in my matching backpack. As I remembered another thing we might need, I added it to my list.

When close friends reached out to ask what they could do to help, I asked them each to bring a new fishing item for him. I placed these in a small tackle box, which I placed with him. I also buried my son with his A-5 shotgun with six shells, his favorite fishing rod, and his play station gear. My father reminded me I still had the ashes of our first hunting dog, Bingo. Bingo died at 11 years old, the number 11 seemed always present in our lives, and we'd had the dog cremated. We placed Bingo with Steven in the casket. It felt better to know Stevo had everything with him including his dog, duck calls, equipment and camping gear, hunting and fishing tools, dog whistle on his lanyard, and a training bumper to work Bingo with on their journey.

I remember how beautiful Stevo's girlfriend, Julie, looked as she performed the song "Dancing in the Sky" in his honor. At times, it still feels like "everything good is missing" since he left. There will always be an emptiness. Some friends have shared videos and photos taken during the funeral. Others have shared video collections of Stevo talking, Stevo swinging, Stevo running. Julie agreed to professionally record the song she sang for my personal collection.

Another special song I remember from the funeral was "Cats in the Cradle" by Harry Chapin. The lyrics talk about how quick time flies between a father and son as the son is growing up. One day, he arrived, and my entire world changed. But then I was busy, flying with my aircraft, then commuting between Memphis and Dover for a few years until Stevo and Pam could join me. That very first time I had to leave my family to go to work in Memphis, Pam prepared a special gift for me from Stevo to remind me who I was doing this for. Although it usually lived on my desk at work, it was in the inside breast pocket of my suit that day, proving itself miraculous at some of my darkest moments. It's still my most cherished possession.

Maybe it is just the bias of a grieving father, but it seemed to me Stevo's funeral was something extraordinary. The numbers of people who attended, the outpouring of support we were given, it all showed the love and respect my son had earned during his short lifetime—across communities, across age groups, across time. His mother Pam, his younger sister Shelby, and myself, Richard Kendrick, will always appreciate the love we felt that day.

To understand what an outstanding young man he was, it will be necessary to tell you all about where he came from, how he got his start in athletics, and how true sportsmanship guided every step he ever took. For Stevo, it was the end of his journey. For the rest of us, it was time to learn how to live without him.

CHAPTER 2: THE WARM-UP

Stevo's athleticism was a natural result of his genes, but his success was his own. His father, me, was a fighter from an early age. In high school, I played football and was on the wrestling team, wrestling my way to district regional and state champion. After graduation, I enlisted in the Air Force as an aircraft mechanic and started wrestling on the base team at Dover AFB. About a year after enlisting, I married a girl I met at a Def Leppard concert.

This was back in 1993, in the days before cell phones when long-distance phone calls were expensive and international calls were even more so. That made it difficult for me to keep in touch with my wife while I was stationed in Italy. My tour of duty was 105 days. My wife and I tried to stay in touch, but we had to coordinate through base times, which made it even more difficult. About halfway through my tour, I received a Dear John letter from my wife saying she was leaving me, but I thought we were still trying to work things out when my tour ended and I went back stateside to my home station. I didn't call ahead because of the expense. Even though no one was expecting me, it was a surprise to come home to an empty house. Concerned, I called around to my wife's family, thinking perhaps she had gone to stay with them for a bit, but they had no idea where she was either. I was becoming more worried by the hour

7

as I tried in vain to figure out where she might be, but she finally turned up a day later at 3 am.

I'd been struggling to get some sleep, when a car playing loud music pulled into the parking lot and a few laughing young adults spilled out. Even though there were two girls and a guy in the car, I had the distinct feeling it was my wife dating the guy, not the other girl.

It was all I could do to keep my cool. She was surprised to see me, as I expected her to be since I hadn't told her I was coming home, but I planned a much happier reunion. I told her if she left again right then, with that other man, we were through.

She and her friend collected her clothes, and they left.

As a young man, 21 years old, I had to go through the trials of divorce and felt the scorn from my friends, family, and acquaintances. I had already called a halt to my wrestling career, but I still worked out and kept in shape. To cope, I spent a lot of time in the sky as a flying crew chief. This meant I was the mechanic that flew with the aircraft on its various missions all over the country. The sky was peaceful, soothing, and didn't contain any judging eyes.

When I was on the ground, I drank. And I fought. Still an angry young man, I lived to take part in drunken skirmishes at bars. In my defense, I usually fought on behalf of the bar, even staying late enough to close the bar and help employees clean up. My motives were not intended to be altruistic, and I wasn't always in the right. I relished the release of the fight and the feeling of power I gained when I won. Bouncers were my best friends, because those were the guys I was always getting in trouble with. Alabama Slammer was my friend, and so was any girl who hung on my arm at the end of the night. I was in the Air Force and had gained that military stance. I was a decent-looking young man. I had my pick of the girls. So, I went down that road for about five or six years.

I know now I was suffering from depression after my first wife left me. I couldn't spend all of my time flying or drunk. To pass the rest of the time, I spent a lot of hours in the garage, working on a frame-off restoration of a '69 Camaro. Everything on that car was brand-new—the restoration, fresh white paint, brand new interior, new engine—I built it all. From the outside, it looked like I was living the life. On the inside, I felt empty. I didn't care about anybody. But then came a night I will never forget.

That night, I'd gotten into a fight, as usual. But this was a bad one. A guy punched me and came down on me with a beer bottle, which broke when I blocked it. The fight left me with my hands all busted up and I still carry scars from that night. The female bartender worried about my condition and asked me to follow her home. It was pouring down rain when I went out to my car. She was standing over by her car, waiting for me, but I was fumbling with my keys. Remember, my hands were all broken up. I dropped the keys and, for some reason, I just started laughing. I remember looking up into the pouring rain, looking up to God.

"Buddy, you can't hurt me anymore," I said. "My heart's broken. I have a wall. I'm stone cold. You can't hurt me now."

I kept laughing as I retrieved the keys, climbed into my Camaro, and went over to that girl's place to continue living life as I had been. It was a few months later that I met Pam.

The night we met started romantically enough. We shared a few dances together and were really hitting it off when, of course, I went and got into another fight. Thanks to my distraction, I failed to get her number that night, but I decided to hang out at that club again to see if maybe I could find her. Sure enough, I went back a week later, and there she was.

I asked her to dance with me again, but she declined. Turned out, she was already there with someone else. There were a lot of lines I would cross back then, but that wasn't one of them. I backed off, going to shoot some pool instead. An hour or so later, one of the cocktail waitresses handed me a slip of paper. It was Pam's number, but she was already gone.

Surprisingly, I didn't get into a fight that night and stayed late to help my buddies, the bouncers and bar staff, clean up. Before we finished, Pam appeared again, knocking at the locked front door. Apparently, she'd told her date she wasn't feeling well and had him take her home early. As soon as he left, she got in her own car and came back for me.

We started dating that night.

Pam was an athlete in her own right. Growing up, she'd been a champion speed skater, winning several regional competitions and a national championship. She'd also been involved in car racing for some time, always fostering an interest in street racing. It was a good thing she'd been in such good shape, as we soon found out.

When Pam found out she was pregnant with Stevo, we had a talk. I told her we were in this relationship and if she wanted to keep the baby, I was there and would do whatever it took. As soon as I found out she was going to have my baby, something in me clicked. Stevo was already bringing about positive changes in me. My first thought was

I had to go back to school. All I'd had was the military. I had my aircraft training from my time in the Air Force, but it wasn't something that I envisioned transferring over to the civilian world. I signed up for classes right away. I'd thought I was closed, cold, no longer vulnerable as I'd told God. God proved to me I still had some squishy middle.

The depth of my love was brought intensely to my attention on the day my son was born. Pam went through several complications that resulted in an emergency C-section, and we almost lost them both. Steven Nicholas Kendrick, named after my baby brother who'd died as an infant, was born on February 9, 1999, at 4:47 pm. He was a healthy 7 pounds, 2 ounces and measured 19 inches.

The moment I held him, that first touch of my son, gave me a flashback to that night in the rain like a slap in the face. I could almost hear God asking me, "are you still so hard? Can nothing hurt you?"

Because of the complications, Pam ended up staying in the hospital for almost a month. It wasn't until they were both healthy, and home, that it finally dawned on me. The Lord proved to me I wasn't as strong or as tough as I thought I was. All I could think in that moment was "You got me, Lord. You got me."

We lived in Dover, Delaware. Pam's job was there, and that's where I was stationed with the Air Force, working on aircraft. Sports was never far away from our lives, even if it was just within earshot. But the family's love for baseball really started when infant Stevo would sit up during feeding times while in the lap of his great-grandfather Popo Steve (my grandfather) to watch the Atlanta Braves game on TV. I'd never played baseball myself, having played football from the Pee-Wee stage all the way through high school. My early experience with baseball turned me off almost immediately. The very first time my dad got me out with a bat and ball, he threw the pitch and it hit me square in the head. That was it, I was done.

Watching baseball together became a ritual for Stevo and Popo. That early exposure had our toddler swinging (and usually connecting) with most anything he could with his baby-sized bat. He broke his first one before he reached the age of two.

"When Stevo first started walking, the first thing he wanted to do was pick up a bat and swing it," Pam said. "He just always wanted to handle a bat and hit a ball. I knew his dad was hoping Stevo would follow in his footsteps with wrestling and football, but baseball was always Stevo's passion."

Even though we never allowed baby talk around him even as an infant, we could never get him to say Pam's sister's name fully even though she lived with us through Stevo's earliest years. He insisted on calling her RaRa, a name she kept from then on, and she remembered him always swinging a bat, too.

"He had a ball pit and while watching TV, he would want you to pitch balls to him so he could swing a bat," RaRa wrote in her journal. "He would say pitch it to me and you would have to do this for a long time."

As soon as he could walk out to the tee, Stevo lived to be on the field. His passion for hitting the ball was clear to everyone. Family photos from Christmas 2000 show him sitting on an inflatable baseball mitt holding a bat with confident glee. Childhood portraits almost always feature Stevo posed with either a baseball bat, football, or basketball. Even at age 2, he was swinging the bat with purpose at the Dover YMCA at Itty Bitty T-ball (noodle ball).

"When we took him to play baseball the first time, it was playing baseball with those pool noodles that kids swim with," RaRa said. "He didn't want to play baseball like that, but he wasn't old enough to play T ball. But when he was able to play T ball, his parents' life was over as they knew it. His father became a coach, and his mom was his #1 supporter, and all the other boys, too. They would fundraise so everyone could afford to play. I loved to see him play the game. He loved it."

By the time Stevo was 3, he had been to major and minor league baseball games, an NFL game, major league hockey, and even saw the Harlem Globetrotters once. We caught him sleeping with his baseball bat in at least one photo, and he always seemed to have a ball in his hands.

When Stevo was born, the bar fights stopped, the drinking stopped, I became a man. I was a father now. I had responsibilities and a family to support. I focused like never before. My position as an aircraft mechanic in the Air Force earned me a position with a crew of mechanics at the huge FedEx hub in Memphis.

The three of us visited the city once in July 2000 for a small family vacation. We spent some time touring through Alabama and visiting some of my family who lived in the Memphis area. With the offer of a good job and all three of us enjoying the city, we decided to try it. I came out first while Pam kept her job in Dover. When I left from the airport that first time, Pam had prepared that miraculous digital card for me from Stevo, a small black square that opened to a photo of my baby boy and a recording of his baby voice, "I love you Daddy," played. Tore at my heart and continues to do so today.

After two years of commuting, just as we were expecting our daughter, Pam and Steven joined me in Memphis. On October 5, 2003, almost four years to the day that Stevo was born, we welcomed Shelby to the family, and our family felt complete. Eventually, I worked my way into management, overseeing all aircraft maintenance at the largest FedEx hub in the world, servicing close to 250 plus flights every 24-hour period.

CHAPTER 3: A SLUGGER'S STORY

U pon moving to Memphis, my life quickly began taking on Stevo's interests and successes. Even at a very young age, even before his sister was born, Stevo was demonstrating uncommon focus and drive, something I noticed and nurtured as much as I could. Like father, like son. Of course, Pam was right, and I was trying to get him involved in other sports, but baseball was always his first love.

On opening day for T-ball at the Kent County Parks and Recreation's April 2002 season, Stevo stepped out on the field for the first true game of his career. At just three years old, he had two at-bats and two runs scored. Our little slugger repeated this record in games two and three that season. By June that year, he'd already improved, getting three at-bats and three runs scored. He continued this record, building up to four at-bats/four runs scored until his last game with three at-bats/three runs scored. It seemed clear to both of us he was a natural at this sport.

To support my son, I turned our garage into a practice gym. By this time, we'd had Shelby, and it was time to give Stevo the support he needed. I constructed a full batting cage within the garage space on one side and used astroturf on the other side to create a space for him to practice fielding ground balls.

This was 2004, the same year I began coaching Stevo's 5's team, the Bartlett Yankees in the Bartlett Park and Rec's league. That year, we had a team of underrated players, including one girl, and together we went all the way to the State Championship game where we finally lost to an all-boys 6-year-old team. That amazing record caught the attention of Jason Evers, whose oldest son played with the Memphis Tigers organization. He told George Mooreland, the president of the organization, about me and our impressive group of youngsters. Mooreland invited me out to lunch after we lost that championship game and offered me a coaching spot, bringing in only the second T-ball team the organization had ever had.

Of course, this meant our daughter, Shelby, never had much choice in sport either. She grew up on the ball field, even taking her first steps at the ballpark. We have so many pictures of her taking her naps in the small wagon we pulled around with us to the various T ball games Stevo was playing and I was coaching. It was never surprising to us when she started showing an interest similar to Stevo's.

While Stevo's intensity about the game was surprising, Shelby's just seemed natural.

As the players developed, so did the garage practice space. The batting cage became capable of soft-toss or fast-pitch practice. I installed a solo-hitter pitching matching, which I equipped with a string tied to the ball so that the ball would always return after it had been hit. Doing it this way made it possible for three batters to be hitting at the same time. Of course, it didn't always work. Today you can still see the holes in the drywall near the back of the garage that resulted from hard-hit balls that missed the net. Each time someone created a new hole, I used a Sharpie to write the batter's name by it for posterity.

I designed the other side of the practice space for fielding practice. I installed artificial turf over the entire floor, with a screen on one end behind the players to protect against missed catches and improve their reflexes. I stood at the other end and hit to them. We trained them to scoop up the ball as quickly as they could, then turn and throw it into the net behind them, and immediately turn back around to be ready for the next one. By doing this, our fielding practice was continuous. Each player got around 40-60 ground balls or pop-ups per practice session.

Once I was coaching a full team, I was all in, coaching spring and winter leagues and holding practice sessions with my players at the house throughout. A player would come to the garage for 30 minutes or an hour of practice time. In the batting cage, they typically got 150-200 cuts per session, three kids at a time. Depending on how long they'd be there or what we needed to work on, they would then switch over to the fielding side. At the end of each practice session, I'd send them home with their parents as the next three were arriving. It was like clockwork: players would walk in through the door, drop their coats and bags, and they went to work. This was par for the course for every team

I coached from those early T ball days all the way through elementary school.

Larry Robinson, one of the baseball instructors from the Dulins Sports Academy, made the comment that I worked these little guys out like a junior college team after watching one of our winter workouts. And he was right. I did. I wore them out in the short time we'd spend together, but they got good at the sport quickly. That garage is where the kids got good at a young, young age. Once they outgrew it, we took it to different indoor facilities. But the garage itself is still full of those memories. The walls are still lined with banners of championship teams whose players practiced inside its walls. One banner lists nine players that went on to play in college.

Besides regular season and the winter league, I typically led a weekend camp for each of my teams once per year. The camps focused on creating unity, camaraderie, and communication within each team. Six full practices filled those weekends, separated by fun events. Each practice took place at a different location, so the team would travel to a different field or facility as the weekend progressed in parent vans and SUVs. That kept the parents there and involved with the team since we needed them to help with the transport.

The team would start out at a specific field specially selected for morning practice, which was usually a hard-running practice. The next practice was usually at an indoor practice facility (once the teams outgrew the garage). This second practice would be something a little less strenuous, such as all hitting. We'd have lunch at a third field in the dugout. While the kids ate, I'd talk with them about dugout rules, team rules, and other team-related or sports-related topics. Then we'd be free to do something fun leading up to dinner and the weekend sleepover party before practices picked up again the next morning. When the practices ended on Sunday, the entire team would attend a special event together, such as motocross or monster trucks. With all this practicing and having fun, we were team building. I was getting my communication in, getting my signs in. I did this with all my boys' teams and, later, my girls' teams.

Doing this, we grew our own little family of baseball families. Michael Robinson was one of those friends, having become part of the family when we invited his son, DJ, to try out for our 6-year-old Memphis Tigers team. DJ was a big kid for his age, so the first time he walked in for tryouts, we thought he was in the wrong place. Michael remembers both myself and Pam telling him the tryouts for the 8-year-old team were on the other side of the gym.

Fearless and undaunted, little DJ hollered out, "I'm only 6."

"They [Richard and Pam] invited DJ in to workout, to tryout, and he made the team," Robinson said. "We were family ever since. It was one of the best relationships we ever had."

Stevo was almost always the smallest one on the team, but Robinson remembers him having the heart of a lion. "You couldn't measure his heart. My son was probably the biggest one on the team, but when it came to the fire inside, Stevo had that from the time you'd hit the field. He was intense—he wanted to get it done. That's who he is, and his intensity drew me to him, and that he wanted to be 'that guy.'"

Perhaps because of that shared spirit, Stevo and DJ bonded right away.

"When we first went to the team, I guess because Steven was smaller than most kids, other kids were picking on him. My son, who's a protector, naturally went to him. DJ's quiet. You never know he's in the room until you mess with somebody he cares about. Then he'll step up and say, 'No, you're not going to do this.' After that, every time they saw each other, there were hugs and just showing love toward one another. When they were playing ball, there was no other place than there watching them play. That went for baseball and football. It was just a joy."

The two boys bounced off each other, continuously pushing each other to be better and do more.

"One thing about Stevo, he hated failure," Robinson continued. "Anything he had to do, whether it was staying late, coming to practice early to get some extra swings in. He wanted to be ready. When the time presented itself for him to be in the batter's box, he wanted that. He wanted probably more than any other kid we had on the team. When it went toward his play, he had this special tenacity. He wanted to hit the baseball so hard and so far. It was like he couldn't wait for the ball to get to him, he had to go get it. He attacked the baseball, both in hitting and handling it. Great hand-eye coordination."

The Robinsons lived in Covington, which meant they had at least a half hour drive every day to practice and a half hour back home. That meant the boys didn't get a lot of time to play together just as friends. However, every time the Robinsons drove through Memphis when they weren't at practice or a game, DJ begged to stop by Stevo's house to go to the batting cage. That, of course, was my oversized garage-turned-practice facility.

"They loved being around each other, they loved being in the cage to see who could hit the hardest," Robinson said. "And it wasn't just the kids who were friends, but the parents. My wife and I, and Pam and Richard, and Richard Baugh and his wife Melisa—there were so many of us. It was more of a family than it was a baseball team. When we did something, we included everybody. It was a wonderful time to spend with Stevo and the Kendricks."

Watching Stevo with DJ and having Robinson and some other dads around was helpful when I came to my first real crisis of conscience regarding my coaching practice and considered quitting.

This was when I was coaching the Memphis Tigers 8's and Stevo was about 7. We were still training in the garage and, of course, Stevo got a lot of that training. My son was full of eagerness to always get better at the game, but he was having a bad night one night, not hitting the ball and letting the frustration get to him. The reason he wasn't hitting was because his form was all jacked up, and I was on him pretty hard about that.

Suddenly, my little boy just started crying. He told me he didn't want to do this anymore, he just wanted to quit. I started getting on him again, and then it hit me. Stevo was the whole reason I was doing this to start with. It had been his passion and his spirit for the game that brought us here. How had we gotten to a point where I was now forcing him to do this from that place where we were doing it because he loved it?

I had to stop everything and regroup. It was time to rethink what I was doing and why. I knew it was his love for the game that brought us here because I had wanted him to wrestle, following in my own footsteps. It hurt me to think I had brought him to a place where now he was crying and wanting to quit this sport he loved. I had to ask myself what I was doing.

That night, I called off the workout early and did a lot of thinking. I talked with some other dads to help me get past my frustration and began to re-evaluate my approach to coaching. It was definitely a learning moment for me. From that moment forward, I became more mindful about the methods I was using and the need to communicate those methods to myself, to the other parents, and to the kids. Out of that moment, I began telling the kids I can be a lot like a light switch.

"If I'm hollering at you," I'd tell them, "it doesn't mean I don't like you. It just means I know you can put in better effort."

I wanted to push them to do their best. But if it wasn't helping them reach their best, I told them I could turn it off, too, because it was important that we had fun.

I had to teach parents and kids about me so they could understand what I was doing and why I was yelling. My son taught me this about myself and also how to deal with it, communicate it better, and why it was important to communicate that.

This teachable moment was another example of how teaching Stevo the game of baseball was teaching me how to coach, and, in a much larger context, how to live.

As the Tigers grew bigger and stronger, and gained more notoriety, I developed a rule of thumb that proved beneficial. People began wanting to play for the Tigers, and suddenly, we were having to turn away players. I had kids coming from all over. During my 10-year-old season, we had two spots to fill and had nearly 40 kids turn up for our try-outs. There were kids showing up who were much better than the kids I already had on the roster. Rather than just slashing the team we'd worked so hard to build, the rule I created was players trying out for the team had to beat our top three. If they came in bigger, stronger, faster, and maybe better athletically than others on the team, but only placed about five or six, it wasn't enough. It wasn't worth it to me to cut kids who'd been with me two, three, or four years, showing up to practice and with parents who had already proven their commitment. That commitment and loyalty meant everything to me. I knew what I was getting with the kids that had been with me. On the other hand, if the new kid could break my top three, I would take that chance for the betterment of the team.

When the time came for elimination, though, it was almost always because of the parents rather than the kids. In all my years of coaching, I only remember letting one player go based on the boy himself. He had issues with respecting the personal space of the others and it wasn't worth the strife, and potential additional issues, that caused. However, I can remember dozens of eliminations I made from the team based on the poor attitudes, lack of commitment, or other issues caused by the child's parents. What made all this success strange was I came into it not knowing much about baseball. It was Stevo himself who taught me everything I knew about coaching. Most of the kids I coached, and very few of the parents, knew I had never played baseball. Many people just assumed I had because I had all those successful teams and had such successful players. I believe what made our teams successful was our work ethic and my own personal spin on the structure of baseball practices. I had a bunch of active little boys with wandering attention spans. And I was coming into this from a wrestling background where repetition in practice was key. I combined my familiar wrestling practice workout style with baseball skills to create a unique approach to baseball practices. This combination and my willingness to adjust and learn from past mistakes allowed for fast-paced practices with multiple reps. Even today, I watch other teams practice and wonder at all the wasted time, Our groups never wasted a minute. All of that started and grew from Stevo.

As successful as our program was, there was only so far I could take my son on my own. By the time Stevo went to middle school, I was bowing out of coaching for the boys. Shelby was turning 6 at about that time, and she needed somewhere she could play softball. Just like I had with Stevo, I put together a team for her and started coaching girls' softball until they turned 12 and heading into middle school. I helped a bit with both kids' middle school teams and, later, with some college exposure coaching, but thought my full coaching days were behind me when Shelby went off to middle school. I wrapped up my last team in 2016.

While that may seem like a wrap on the story, it is just the bare bones of the system. Along the way, we developed into a traveling tournament team, achieving national recognition, and learning so many unexpected lessons along the way. These are the kinds of things we wish we'd learned when our kids were small, before we embarked on the journey.

CHAPTER 4: TOURNAMENT FAMILIES AND DISNEY

When your athletic children dedicate themselves to playing at the year-round tournament level, sports quickly dominates your life. You work; you come home; you do sports; you go to bed. Traveling to the next new game or tournament fills each weekend. There is very little time off for friends or family outside of sports, so the team becomes your family. That's the way it was for us, and that's the way it is for hundreds of families playing the circuits in hopes of a college scholarship someday or just in pursuit of playing the best game they can play. Our pursuit of that best game came in the form of the Disney Invitational.

Disney World's Wide World of Sports Invitational is what is known as a Super Elite 24 Invite event. This means it invites only the top 24 teams in the country. Not only that, but you have to play in specific tournaments during the year to get the rankings needed. Not just any tournament will do. It wasn't just the accolades and pride associated with being among the top 24 elite teams in the country that excited us. We'd also have the opportunity to play on the gorgeous fields featured in the ESPN Wide World of Sports campus videos and websites. And we'd be in Florida, staying in one of the Disney World resort hotels with the ability to take our young families to the famous amusement park outside of game and practice time.

For most of our families, the 9-year-old boy on our team was the oldest child in the household. Because of all the expenses associated with being on an elite team, most of these families didn't have the finances to take their entire families for lavish vacations like this. Because of our dedication to sport, none of us had time for vacations such as this. It was one of those hard lessons in life you can't go back to fix. Without later wisdom to guide us, this seemed a win-win-win-win situation.

Stevo was already a starter for the team by the time we put Disney in our long-range sights. His heart of a champion really lit up that season as a team leader. The dynamic of the formation of tight bonds made during travel seasons cannot be underestimated. It explains how Stevo's view of the world was shaped from an early age. One way in which this manifested was his seemingly innate second nature to do for others.

"We noticed that Stevo liked to help others very early on," Pam said. "When he played ball, he'd go in the dugout and give people his stuff to use. He was the child that would share whatever he had. If they didn't have it, he'd make sure they'd get it. It wouldn't be unusual for others to have his equipment."

In terms of how close the traveling teams and their parents grew, Pam explains: "You spend a lot of time with these people, not only practicing with them a couple days a week but you travel with them, you stay in hotels with them, you eat with them, you're at the ballpark with them. So, you become a really close-knit group of people. They become part of your family. Kendrick always used to say something that I never put perspective on until Stevo got much older. With him being the coach, he'd say, 'The kids are great. I'll cut a parent before I'll cut a kid.' He thought it was important for the atmosphere to be just as good on the field as off the field."

To foster that inclusive atmosphere, we created the 24-hour rule for parents. They were always welcome to talk with me about their concerns, but had to wait 24 hours after the event or situation that upset them. This usually involved things such as playing time, a specific circumstance or play, or something another kid might have said on the field. It's easy for parents to get caught up in the heat of the moment during their kids' sporting event, especially when you play at the tournament level. I didn't want to get caught up in the emotions or have those emotions affecting the team. However, if they were still upset about it 24 hours later, it was important to clear the air. I never allowed a discussion during game times or tournament play. That rule was hard and fast.

"So all the parents got along great," Pam continued. "There wasn't a lot of animosity. If there was something disagreeable, we'd just go separate ways. Don't get me wrong, we wanted to be good—that's what travel ball is about. At the same time, if you have someone putting wedges or there's one bad apple in the group, it can destroy the on-field play as quick as it can off field. You surround yourself with people that are all out for the same goal, not for any individual praise. You build from that."

The Baughs were definitely on board with that concept. As the team traveled to tournaments from Little Rock to Cooperstown and places in between in caravans with Memphis Tigers flags hanging out the windows, everyone knew I was all about playing the best competitions and putting our boys in the best light. They also knew I wouldn't put up with any parents causing trouble in the group. That meant everyone worked together to keep things positive and proactive for the team.

For each travel weekend, Pam would book the hotels with rooms in blocks. That way, we could keep the team together in one area, which made it feel more like one big family.

"On the door of each family's room she had a cardboard cutout baseball with that player's number," Melisa Baugh said. "The boys would have a great time in-between games, coming home from the games, running up and down the hotel hallways."

While the other hotel guests may not have agreed, we tried to instill some discipline even while fostering this fun traveling atmosphere.

"Then there was bed check," Richard Baugh said. "We were all going to have fun, but it was all about playing some ball. So, by 10 p.m., those boys better be bathed and in bed, because Kendrick was going to come in and tell them goodnight. Well, Kendrick had a military background, so it made sense. It was a tight ship, but we all had great times.

"It couldn't have been more like a family. Kendrick and Pam ran it, and it was so well organized. It was all open—all the finances, communication, everything. We did fundraisers. All of us would do Thanksgiving dinners together, Christmas dinners together, every year. And Pam would always do something special for all the team mothers on Mother's Day; she would have all the boys present their mothers with gifts like flowers. Then they'd do something on Father's Day. It was just one big family.

"People did come and go, but we had a core group of about nine of us who were as tight knit as you'd see."

The 2008 summer travel season took the Memphis Tigers family to some great wins as they marched their way toward Disney. The 9's team had already won a fair share of the games they'd played, but it was playing in the Super NIT in Birmingham, Alabama, that would decide the outcome. Win this last tournament and they went to Disney.

Pam kept a team scrapbook documenting our progress that year, pulling together articles I wrote for the games and website:

The Memphis Tigers traveled to Birmingham, AL, chasing the dream—the Tigers had set their goals high this season and the Road to Disney was the Dream. This meant becoming a member of the Elite 24 field that would compete in Orlando at the Wide World of Sports Complex at Walt Disney World and be among the top 24 teams in the nation. What would this take? It would require a Super NIT Championship.

The Tigers arrived late Friday afternoon and would draw the late game (9 p.m.) against Rascal Baseball. The Rascals would throw their big ace all night against the Tigers. The Tigers found a few holes, but the big #25 Brooks would keep the Tigers off balance all night. One of the best pitchers the Tigers have seen this year.

Saturday morning brought more heartache for the Tigers, as the Alabama Attack [the #1 USSSA team in the nation] and Line Drive Baseball sent the Tigers to the bottom of the seeding. The Tigers just could not get anything going and got a taste of what big-time baseball teams are about. To compete at this level, you cannot take a pitch off. The Tiger coaches and players would have a mindset meeting after the 3rd loss of pool play. The Tigers wouldn't get to go swimming after the 3rd loss until they hit the practice field. Coach Kendrick and Trainor wouldn't let the boys leave until the Tigers knew what 100% meant and how to finish. Something happened in that session as the boys became a new team. On Sunday, Mother's Day, a different Tiger baseball team would take the field.

The Tigers were at the bottom of the pack with a #10 seeding, which put the Tigers in the first game of the day, 8 a.m. against #7 seed Oxford Bombers. The Tigers would jump out quick with 6 runs in the first. The Tiger defense did the rest. 7-5 Tigers. The Tigers would then advance to face #2 seed Line Drive Baseball. The Tigers knew this would be a hard-fought game, as these two teams have gone toe-to-toe each time they have met. DJ Robinson would take the mound first, with Chris Swanberg coming in and closing the door on Line Drive with some ace pitching. 8-6 Tigers, advancing to semi-finals.

The Tigers would face the #3 seed TPSA Bandits. The Tigers would jump out with some solid hitting and defense to take a commanding lead 9-2 going into the bottom of the 6th. The Tigers were three outs away from the championship game, not so fast!

The hard-hitting Bandits were not ready to just let the Tigers walk up the hill to the championship game. The Bandits strung together a few singles and then a grand slam and another solo home run! The Bandits had battled back and tied the game.

The mental toughness of the Tigers showed as the international rules came into play. Hayden "The Hammer" Leatherwood would crush a single to center and drive in the two runs. DJ Robinson would come in and get the save and put the Tigers in the championship game. Tigers 11-9.

Memphis Tigers vs Gulf Coast Lightening: The Tigers would win the toss, thanks to DJ calling tails, and the Tigers would be the home team for the first time all day. William Locke would take the mound and pitch three flawless innings. DJ Robinson would get the scoring started for the Tigers with a two-run 200+ ft home run over left-center field. Garrett Baugh would come in and close the game, pitching the last three innings. Tigers 6-4 (SUPER NIT CHAMPIONS).

This group proved what they could accomplish when you believe in yourself and each other. This is what a Team is all about!!! The Tigers' backs were against the wall, and all odds were against them. The Tigers learned a lot from other teams this weekend on what being a team means. Hat's off to all the great times in the Tournament.

The Tigers had won a berth as one of the USSSA National Elite 24 "Road to Disney." The boys all claimed they did so for their moms. They were now one of the top 10 teams in the nation, setting new sights on Orlando, where they would play in August.

May that year was a busy, exhausting month, but it was successful. It was the mid-point of the season and the Tigers had brought home hardware from all but one tournament, resulting in four championships, two consolation championships, and one runner-up.

We took those boys to the Elite 24 at Disney, playing all the top teams in the country.

But before we got to the fields, we had a little time for each family to enjoy what was, for some of them, their first taste of the Florida beaches. I was worried some of them would overindulge.

Knowing everyone was excited about the vacation to Florida, I told the team, "Okay, we're going down there, and we're going to have a practice to warm up before our first game."

Of course, it was one of the core group that proved my worry was well-founded. Kevin "Shane" Cochran, his wife Sonya, and son BamBam (Seth) were part of our close-knit core group of families, having been with the team from our first group of 6-year-olds.

When it came to racking up the mileage to various and sundry games for the traveling teams, it was always us tagging up together with the Cochrans to get things moving. I met Shane, who would become my assistant coach, at the ballpark. Living in nearby Atoka, Shane was a career firefighter with the Shelby County Fire Department. Before moving to Atoka ("God's country" as he related to friends), when the kids were younger, he had started a baseball league with the kids in the neighborhood, each team only having two players.

We became best friends. Pam became best friends with Sonya. Stevo and BamBam were inseparable. We lived on the road together; traveling, training, working these boys out like it was junior college. We spent all our time together, in hotels every weekend, raising money, trying to figure out how to save money. If I could have all that money back, I could have sent my boy to any Division 1 school we wanted in the country. I couldn't fault them for taking a tiny mini vacation in the couple of days leading up to the tournament.

On practice day, though, little BamBam Cochran showed up looking like a lobster, sunburnt from head to toe. He was our star catcher. All I could think was what are you doing?! He couldn't possibly wear his full catcher's gear with a burn like that. But these were 9-year-old boys, what're you going to do? Poor kid could barely move he was so sun-burnt, and couldn't practice for the first 48 hours of the tournament.

BamBam's sunburn wasn't our only or biggest disappointment going into the Disney tournament. The let-down started with our 'resort' hotel, which wasn't bad, but it also wasn't much different from any of the other hotels we'd stayed in to get to this point. The same beige walls, the same generic patterned bed covers, the same basic furnishings. The kids were expecting to see Mickey and Minnie wandering the lobby, but there was none of that. There may have been a few Disney details that have faded with the passing of time, but it certainly wasn't enough of a splash to stick in anyone's memory as a unique or magical experience.

To get to this point in our pursuit of the dream, we had played in some truly beautiful ballparks all across the country. Like the hotel, we expected the pinnacle of our season to be something fabulous, something that would symbolize for all of us the magnitude of our accomplishment.

In the spirit of the payoff being worth the effort, our expectations only grew bigger as we made the mile and a half trek, toting all of our equipment and younger kids, to our practice and playing fields. That first time, we walked with fortitude, our minds filled with the visions we'd gleaned from the online images, the beautiful fields we'd played on so far, and the anticipation of the big build-up to this moment.

It was shocking to us to find, at the end of the journey, one of the worst fields we'd seen all season. I think the boys were perhaps more disappointed than the parents.

The adults did everything we could to play up what a wonderful achievement it had been for the boys to get us there, but the complete experience didn't live up to the crowning memory for the boys we expected. It ended up being a significant bucket list item we could now check off, but we never attempted to go back. It was that much of a let-down. By now, we had the experience to know which events to pursue that would give our kids the experience we wanted them to have.

The Tigers played in Orlando on August 3, placing No. 17 in play, and ranking #5 overall of the Elite 24 teams. They earned an overall USSSA record of 47-22. Not a bad year for the Tigers having finished the season with 64 total wins.

At that point, the Memphis Tigers were ranking number 2 nationwide and, as it turned out, had their true crowning glory still ahead of them. Shane helped me coach the Memphis Tigers 10 group all the way to Cooperstown, NY, a mecca for any baseball fan. The kids stayed in barracks with the coaches. Our entire time there was dedicated exclusively to baseball. It was an amazing event overall and a beautiful complex. To us, this was the pinnacle for youth sports we'd envisioned. We returned a few years later with the 12-year-old group.

Going into our 11-year-old season, we had such a big turnout of kids trying out for the team, we divided them into two teams—the Memphis Tiger Green team, the A club, and the Memphis Tiger Gold, the B or C club. For the organization, it was another way to raise funds to support our traveling expenses. For the kids, it was a way to give more hopeful players a chance to play for a recognized organization. Playing for the Tigers was $100 a head off the top, just to wear the name. So, every team member I had was paying $100 a pop just to be on the roster. This expense didn't include the required uniforms or everything else that goes into playing on a team. The expenses add up quickly and, for some parents, the pressure to keep up can be more than anyone outside might realize.

CHAPTER 5: SEASONS OF TRAGEDY

· ·

The price of the road can be high. Just ask anyone who spends most of their time on it. This is no different whether you are a star musician or a star team of elementary-school-age children. We don't always realize how high that price can be until the bill comes due.

For us, that shocking reality came to full light in 2009, just as we reached the pinnacle of our success. Shane had been my assistant coach for about four years, riding alongside me for every practice, every game, every success we'd had as often as he could. As a firefighter, there were times he didn't have control over his shift time. But we were close enough friends that his firefighter buddies had even invited me out a time or two, hanging out with them at their favorite spot to unwind after a particularly grueling shift or especially troubling week. It was just a non-descript spot in an isolated place next to a railroad line where they'd break out the beers, and sometimes stronger drinks, and vent about work, life, and all things troubling them.

By the time we got back from Cooperstown that first time, I also knew Shane was going through some tough times. Since we were friends and did all this traveling together, we'd compared notes the way guys do—money is tight, relationships seem distant, typical stuff most parents go through. The pressure of work, finances, and his personal life were beginning to show, but I didn't realize how deep they went. I was working the night shift at FedEx at the time and expected to have a relatively quiet night on the Fourth of July, but I got a hysterical call from Sonya at about 2 am. The news was devastating and sent me into a downward spiral it took years to recover from.

Apparently, Shane had been out on the golf course all day with some friends. By the time he got back home, Sonya was upset. The two of them got into an argument. Sonya mentioned his drinking that day. Shane went to that isolated place near the railroad tracks where his firefighter co-workers often went. It's probable he had more to drink while there and somehow ended up on the tracks themselves. The train bells and horns started blaring in the distance, the tracks started rumbling, and the clanging bells at a nearby crossroads all encouraged him to move. According to the train conductor, though, he was still struggling to get off the tracks by the time the train overtook him. He was only 36 when he died on July 5, 2009.

Once I got off the call with Sonya, I called Pam to share the news with her and headed over to the Cochran's house to do what I could. I accessed the accident scene just two days after Shane's death. I went with another dad from the team, Richard Baugh. Both of us were shaken by the event and needed some way to feel closure. It was a time we will never forget. Time seemed to stand still as we contemplated what had happened.

Shane was a much-loved personality in several circles. He left a void we would feel for quite some time afterward. Myself, Stevo, and the other families on the team mourned for months.

Meanwhile, we had scheduled the team to play in the Gulf USA World Series championship tournament in Gulf Shores. The tournament took place just a week after Shane's death. I had these 10- and 11-year-old boys and their parents looking to me for guidance and support when I was feeling devastated myself. I pulled them all in and had that talk with them. We had to set everything up, get Shane buried. We—the whole team—spent a lot of time there with Sonya. And we had to decide what we were going to do about the tournament.

All the parents wanted us to still play in the tournament. Our Pitching Coach Mike Wheat stepped up in a big way even though he didn't have a child on the team. But his presence and help in filling the roles needed for every family member was crucial. We were all grieving, but he stepped up to make sure we all had what we needed. I hope he knows how much he meant to each of us. I still feel so much love for this man.

We knew making it to the tournament would be a tight squeeze, but we spent extra time planning everything to be as respectful to our fallen assistant coach and still honor his memory by fulfilling our obligations and goals. We left straight from the funeral to drive down to Gulf Shores and play. Shane's son BamBam rode down with me. Pam and I were his godparents. We were all just so close. We went down to Gulf Shores and won that tournament USSSA World Series Championship.

At that game, Franklin Hefflinger (aka Turtle) pitched a game like he never had before. As we were losing, Turtle used a speed pitching technique we'd practiced to perfection. Our original thought was to use it when we needed quick outs as time was running out, but we needed the last at bat. It drove other coaches crazy as it completely exposed any of their stall tactics, and it flattered batters. Turtle did this to give our team a chance. It was the chance that gave us the edge and allowed us to pull off another trip to championship levels when all odds were against us. However, this year, it was the last game of the season.

As it turned out, that would also be one of the last times I would be associated with the Memphis Tigers. Things weren't the same after Shane's tragic passing. I'd never been a particularly strong man before Stevo entered my life and gave me purpose. By this point in life, though, being a parent felt a little routine. It was the friendships I shared with other dads that kept me focused on the right thing. With the loss of my best friend, I felt adrift. Like Shane, my relationship with Pam had become something closer to a business relationship as we tried to manage all the details that went into running an elite team like ours. Shane's passing and Sonya's grief just added that much extra to our already full plates. But we weren't done dealing with tragedy yet.

On October 18, 2010, a year and some months after Shane's accident, 50-year-old Chastain Montgomery and his 18-year-old son Chastain Montgomery Jr. drove down from Nashville to the Henning Post Office. The older Montgomery had once worked as a janitor at that post office. It was also where Paula Robinson, DJ's mother, was working that morning. The two Montgomery's hopped over the counter and demanded money from the cash register. Montgomery senior later admitted that he 'lost it' because there was only $63 in the drawer.

The two men took out their rage on the female postal workers, opening fire on both women and striking them each multiple times. Paula Robinson was just 33 years old. The other victim was 59-year-old Judy Spray. After trying unsuccessfully to get more money from the safe, the Montgomery pair fled.

The double murder was just the start of a six-month-long crime spree. Law enforcement caught up with the younger Montgomery after a high-speed chase involving a carjacked vehicle. Junior was gunned down while exiting the car and shooting at police. They arrested the elder Montgomery and the federal court sentenced him in 2014 to two consecutive life sentences without the possibility of parole.

"No sentence can pay for the loss of a loved one, but we hope this prosecution has helped bring some sense of closure to the victims' families," said Assistant Attorney General Caldwell.

Added U.S. Attorney Edward Stanton, "The senseless and heinous murders of Paula Robinson and Judy Spray have left an irreplaceable void throughout the entire community. The life sentence without the possibility of parole imposed upon Chastain Montgomery, Sr. today will hopefully bring justice and a meaningful measure of closure to the Spray and the Robinson/Croom families."

"People say time heals, but time doesn't heal," Michael Robinson said in an interview just before the publication of this book. "It's been nine years now. Time teaches you how to deal with it, but you don't heal from something that's so tragic to someone you love so much. You learn how to deal with it on a daily basis."

Without the strong foundation of my fellow fathers from the team, I began making several poor decisions of my own. Over the next three or four months, I began spending more and more time with another woman associated with the team. The relationship deepened quickly and without realizing it or even trying, I found myself spending as much time with her as I could. It was her, rather than my wife, who I turned to when Paula was murdered.

Of course, it didn't take long for the team to find out about the affair. The boys were 12. It disappointed the parents. Pam was furious, hurt, betrayed, humiliated. There was no coming back from that, and the Memphis Tigers moved in another direction. Looking back, I'd been coaching with the organization for about six years by then. Even without the extra pressures, it would have been normal for them to move to another coach.

I made one last stand coaching boys with a team called the Memphis Travelers, but only lasted a few months. With parents knowing about my affair with another team mom while going through the motions of a divorce from Pam, everybody ejected.

As if I wasn't low enough, I could feel that Stevo, while he still seemed to respect me, wanted to be better than me in every facet of life. I knew my boy loved me, and we had a friendship like no other, but he also saw that I hurt his mom when I had the affair. I was terrified of losing my kids. Mercifully, Pam decided to try working things out with me. Instead of following through on the divorce proceedings, once I quit the affair, she allowed me to stay in the house with the rest of the family as we tried to work things through.

With a year's break from the full-time stress of coaching a traveling team, with the aftermath of the affair behind us, and with Shelby now playing softball, it was time for me to get busy with my next project.

Like Stevo, Shelby started playing T-ball at a nearby community youth ballpark. She had fun and made friends but was quickly outgrowing the competition thanks to her experience and early exposure. This is a common issue for girls. Lots of talent, not so much opportunity. I wasn't willing to let that happen for my little girl.

When it came time to coach Shelby, I decided that no one was going to control my fate anymore. I would not have an organization or anyone telling me I can or cannot coach. If I was going to do it, it was going to be on my terms.

I approached Gene Harrison at the Bolton ballpark to ask if he'd consider bringing a girls' team under The Bolton Wildcats organization. Gene Harrison was the president of the Bolton Youth Organization at the time and is in the Tennessee Hall of Fame as a youth coach. With his acceptance and guidance, and the opportunities he kept opening in front of me, I launched into creating a structure for my little girl. Even while I was busy coaching Shelby's 6-year-old team, I was building an entire sports organization from the ground up for her to grow into.

We began going to watch older teams play, building relationships with other families, and recruited players in Shelby's age group from there to create her own competitive level team. Then we began recruiting players to form a second team, doing so by talking with a coach and getting my hands on the roster. These girls were raw, but athletic. They were fast runners, but they'd always been relegated to recreational players. Their skill level had a lot of room for growth before they would meet with my standards. I met with the parents and soon held a clinic to raise money for Shelby. Approximately 60 girls, all older than Shelby, came to the camp. As I worked with the players, I could see the parents were appreciating the fact that someone was offering their girls higher level coaching than what had been available to them. Soon, parents were asking me how their daughters could come play for us.

Now that the parents were bringing their daughters for evaluation, the team roster quickly filled up. That season featured my 6-year-old team with Shelby and a 10-and-under team, both brimming with talent. We had so much talent, in fact, that the 6-year-old girls played in a fall baseball league, and the boys didn't want to play them. We beat half the league. It hurts a coach's feelings when he's got boys getting beat by little girls. They didn't like that at all.

With just the two teams, we would go to a tournament, play our games, then I would watch teams playing in other age ranges. When I saw a team that was obviously well-coached with a lot of talent, I would approach the players on those independent teams to inquire whether they would be interested in playing for the (then) Lady Wildcats. This was how I built the organization, from the 6-year-olds to the 18-year-old youths, for the girls.

But I was struggling to get the talent. People within youth sports tended to associate the Bolton name as a local community ball club. While there was nothing wrong with that, we were having some trouble gaining recognition on a national level which, in turn, restricted our recruiting opportunities. I knew if I wanted better ball players, I had to change the name to something that would be more recognized in the national circuits. And to do that, I needed a sponsor.

Talking with the head of the boys' side of the organization—the Bolton Wildcats—I laid out my plan for changing names across the organization, which would include updating uniforms, signage, and other elements of team identification. The Bolton Wildcats had eight ball clubs. Turned out, they were also struggling to attract the talent they wanted, so they agreed.

That's when I contacted Rawlings and Worth. I asked them what it would take to use their name. I signed a deal with those guys, and that's when things started to change. Just like that, the existing boys' team changed to the Rawlings Prospects. The earlier Lady Wildcats became the Worth Prospects. At our peak, we had 23 teams.

As director, I soon settled into my new role as "soother." Ironically, perhaps, I was the one who soothed situations and kept the off-the-field antics of coaches and parents muted. My primary goal was to keep off-the-field drama from affecting the teams so they could continue to compete unfettered and not distracted. I had coaches who were stealing money, parents who were having affairs, the list goes on.

Like the Disney trip, I didn't know what I was getting into, the dynamics of overseeing something so big, or the repercussions it would have down the road. If I could have had just the kids there, it would've been great.

The organization grew too big too fast. We couldn't control it. With 10 girl teams, I had coaches that would quit last minute or just not show up. Who steps in when that happens? I had to, because I had no one else in place to help. Shelby would get mad, and rightfully so, because I'd be coaching her, and we might be up six runs, but I'd have to leave mid-game to coach another team that didn't have a coach. I was just everywhere.

Steven became my biggest fan, best assistant coach, and game strategist. We always talked about the game. I taught him players were like chess pieces. You had to understand the players strengths and weaknesses in order to position them in the right places. It was my firm belief we could take the losing team, coach to their strengths and shore up their weaknesses, and go on to beat any team. We broke everything down: speed, power, pitch selection based on a batter's stance or where they stood in the box. To love the game as we did was to become master of the game. Stevo shared this passion and wanted to learn every aspect of how I was coaching down to the smallest detail. The debates we had were wonderful as we explored ideas late into the night.

The last year I coached, I coached 414 games. To coach that much, I had no choice but to stay on the night shift at work. I can remember one weekend when, after getting off my Friday evening shift (which meant it was 5 am on Saturday morning), I drove straight to the ballpark. My first game that day started at 8 am and my last game ended at 9 pm that night, coaching all the way through. When the team I was coaching was winning, I'd notice another team struggling and bounce over to that game. To no one's surprise, I ran myself into the ground.

This frantic pace as the organizational director and multi-team coach lasted for two years before I finally stepped down. Pam and I were supposed to be trying to work things out during this time, but really, I was spending most of my time at work, on the ball field, or sleeping on the couch. After all this time had passed, it was time to acknowledge there was no repairing the situation, but neither of us seemed able to step forward and make it a reality.

Of course, Stevo saw everything going on. One day he approached me and asked, "Dad, why are you sleeping on the couch every night?"

I told him I was there for him and his sister. I told him how important they both were to me and asked him not to worry about me. As long as I had them, I didn't need anything more.

Stevo said, "No Dad, you're good. You don't have to sleep on the couch."

It was like my boy gave me permission to get out of that situation. My son was maturing as a man, tired of seeing his parents hurting and ready to take the lead. I realized while my marriage was over, I would never stop being father to my kids. So, I moved out and got my own apartment until our renters' lease was up on our original house.

The divorce that followed and the need to pay child support led me to take a promotion to a lead position at FedEx. I worked the day shift briefly while transitioning, but continued to work nights for another three years before taking over as manager of aircraft maintenance on the day shift full time.

It was like something I heard one time from my grandfather: 'You'll have everything you always wanted in life, then you'll lose it all. Then you'll need to build it back up again. You may lose it all again, and you've got to start over.' When it came to my son's ball and my daughter's ball,

I took them both to the highest peak, and I lost it all. After the Memphis Tigers with Stevo, I took it back up with Shelby. And I lost it all again.

When Stevo lived at Pam's with Shelby, his leadership in the house after the divorce meant he had to grow up fast.

"But there was no pressure on either of them," Pam said. "My goal was for them to just be kids. We always laughed and called him the man of the house. He would take care of the 'man things' around the house. If something needed fixed, he usually couldn't fix it, but he'd try."

This was where Stevo elevated himself from talented athlete to Sports Star.

CHAPTER 6: RAISING SPORTS STARS

. . . .

The difference between talented athletes and sports stars is all about attitude. Having the determination to go on, the leadership to encourage others, and the wisdom to know when to fall back. Being the natural athlete that he was, baseball wasn't the only sport Stevo excelled in. Toward the end of his elementary school days, he started playing basketball, too. As all coaches do, Coach Barrlow first started noticing Stevo in fifth grade. He knew he had a pretty good incoming 6th grade class and led a five-day basketball summer camp that summer that Stevo attended.

"I remember telling Coach Brooks about halfway through camp, 'I know I've got one player coming,'" Barrlow said, remembering Stevo. "He had a very competitive mindset that you want to see, diving after loose balls, just playing hard, competitive basketball. Of course, that carried on with the other sports he took on. The relationship started there."

The reputation that proceeded Stevo was always proven out during his play.

"When he came in, he had the fundamental skills, ball handling, passing, good shooting form, and what we look for at that age, putting up layups right- and left-handed," Barrlow continued. "But he was going to get better, he was going to make sure of that. Again, it was his mindset. It was personal for him. It didn't matter who he was competing against, he was going to be the best he could be. And so, his skills got better because he was going to will it to be."

At times, coaches touch base with their student athletes during the school day. Kids often will bring whatever is going on at home to school. Good coaches want to reach out to see if things are going okay, to get a feel for their mentality as a season progresses. Coach Barrlow never had to touch base with Stevo.

"That's one of the best attributes about Stevo. Once that ball was tossed in the air, the game was on. He was focused, driven. You never had to question where his mindset was going to be, whether he was going to be ready come game time. The problem was, was he going to be over-ready? And that's playing through whatever the situation was."

In fact, that competitive spirit nearly took him out of all games. It was during one of these basketball games in 8th grade when Stevo's career almost ended. The team was in a regional championship game, and Stevo was determined not to leave anything home.

"We were playing Haywood," Coach Barrlow said. "I didn't tell the kids we had already won the regular-season championship, but I really wanted to beat Haywood, so I just told the players that this would sew us up for the district and put us where we wanted to be. We led for most of that game, but it got tight by the fourth quarter. Then I saw Stevo grimace clutching his shoulder and thought, 'Oh man.' I saw Dad come from the other side, and they were over there working and working."

From where I was sitting, I could see what was happening on the court clearly. Stevo got locked up with another player on the court, each going opposite directions. When they came down, it was Stevo's shoulder that gave way. When they carried him over to the sidelines, I could see that his shoulder had gone down into his left pectoral muscle. It wasn't looking good. Security came, and we moved him to under the bleachers to avoid upsetting anyone in the crowd. It was gruesome. All I could think of to do was give him a hug as I tried to figure out the next best move. Should we wait for the school nurse to help, call for paramedics, drive him to the hospital, what?

The moment seems to stretch out in my memory.

As I hugged him, I looked down at his pain-filled face. His eyes rolled back as I squeezed, and I thought he had just passed out. It's possible he lost consciousness for a moment as I felt his shoulder slip beneath my arms, quietly popping back into place as he tried to hug me back.

Happiness bloomed across his face and he had such a sweet smile as he uttered the words, "I love you, Dad." Stevo had such a sweet smile on his face. He was so grateful that his shoulder returned to its socket. It clearly felt better immediately.

This is such a cherished memory for me, the moment I was able to fix his pain.

Of course, while I was still clinging to the moment, all Stevo wanted to do at that point was head back into the game. I knew my son. I knew his tenacity. I had no choice but to let him go. The coach looked a little dubious as well, looking over at me, but seemed to come to the same conclusion I had.

"I looked at his dad and said, 'It doesn't matter whether he has to go through you and me, he's going back in.' That's a good example of his mindset. You can't teach that. That's innate, that's God-given, that's internal. If you could teach it, every coach would do it, but you can't give anybody that."

The shoulder continued to pop in and out of place for the rest of the game, which was thankfully almost over, anyway. We found out later all the muscles and ligaments surrounding his shoulder joint had come out, some torn. Stevo had to have complete reconstructive surgery on it. He worried he'd miss his freshman year of baseball because of it.

Fortunately, it was his left shoulder that was injured, his non-throwing arm. He was in a sling for about two months and was extra-disciplined about following through on his physical therapy. Just before baseball workouts began for his freshman team, his doctor declared him to be 99% recovered. He told Stevo he could never make him as God had created him, but he'd repaired it as close to perfection as it could be. Stevo never missed a beat baseball-wise and went on to have a strong freshman year.

Coach Barrlow has been coaching basketball and football since 2004 and has since added tennis, but says he's never encountered another athlete quite like Stevo.

"Stevo was at the top when it came to competing, when it comes to anything I've coached," he said. "He's at the top of the list. He came with competitiveness, toughness. If I could put a personality in my players, it would be his."

It was the sign of Stevo's toughness and my tenacity to get him through such moments, teaching him how to push through and find a way.

Meanwhile, baseball continued on. At the tournament level, it's always one game after another, always pushing to the next tournament, the next championship, the next level. That's the life of an athlete's family, and it was no different for us. Dozens of trophies, plaques, and other hardware still fill a room at Pam's house. Although our location in the tri-state region was a natural gathering point for competitive sports of all types from Mississippi, Arkansas, and Tennessee, all strong, athletic states, it was always Stevo's natural-born leadership that stood out.

"I never realized how much of a true leader he was until later, until now," Pam said. "I always saw his leadership on the field. I always saw his motivation to other players. I saw him stick up for kids here and there, but the way he touched people was so much deeper than I ever knew. I have strangers coming up to me and sharing stories of how they met Steven, what he did for them, things I didn't even know."

One example was when a boy whom Shelby knew from school approached us at church one night after Stevo's passing. He asked for a ride to Wal-Mart where his parents were. On the way there, I asked him where he had met Stevo, and the boy responded, "On the school bus." Stevo hadn't ridden the bus since middle school. Yet, it was on the bus where the boy was being bullied, and Stevo offered to sit with him so the others would leave him alone.

"He was a protector, too," Pam said. "He was this boy's friend then all the way through high school."

And it was during middle school (5th-8th grade) that Stevo befriended Chase Suggs. They both played baseball and basketball, and both families joined the larger "family" of traveling athletes as we spent countless hours (and countless miles) as traveling teams. By being the leader he was, Steve inspired other players to bring out their A game and keep playing on.

Another example of Stevo's quiet leadership was a player that went to baseball camp one year who wouldn't eat the camp lunch because he didn't like it. When his dad picked him up, knowing he would be hungry, he asked him where he wanted to go eat. The 9-year-old boy told his dad he wasn't hungry because one of the other players shared his McDonald's lunch. That was Stevo, who was a senior at the time and could get an outside lunch.

Once Steven got to about 14, I realized I had peaked out with him and he needed different coaching for his exposure years. He rejoined the Memphis Tigers as a 14-year-old, playing for Coach Griggs and Coach Chris Stewart on the tournament circuit for greater college exposure. Stevo was influential in bringing Nick Johnson onto that team as well. The two had already been friends for years. Nick had an absent father and had traveled with me and Stevo through our own traveling ball days. Their relationship endured even as they went to their individual schools, and it was Stevo who got Nick back involved enough to play through high school graduation and into the college scene.

Even from his youngest days, one of Stevo's most outstanding attributes was his competitive nature. This was something Coach Harrison noticed early on. You might remember Coach Harrison was and is the President of the large Bolton Athletic Association, a Tennessee Coaching Hall of Famer, and the man who gave me a chance to build a system for my daughter to grow up in. At any given time,

15-20 teams participated at Bolton Park, with its five ball fields, and Coach Harrison would move around and interact with the teams and the parents. When Stevo outgrew my coaching abilities, I approached Coach Harrison to ask about whether there was a spot for Stevo within his organization.

"He was actually a year younger than the team I was coaching, the 11-year-olds," Coach Harrison remembers. "I would take the players from 11 to 14, then drop back down to 11 and back up to 14, until they went to high school. I ran into Richard and he wanted to bring out some girls' softball teams; this was when his little girl was playing softball up north of us. We opened up an area for them to practice and play."

This was the field the parents and I cleared out and prepared for our girls. We were so grateful to have not only the place to practice, but the organization to associate with. I was impressed with the entire program they had running there, partially informed by Stevo's experience with another team in the group. Even though I knew Coach Harrison was working with an older group of boys, I believed he could give Stevo some pointers I didn't think he would get anywhere else.

"At the time, Stevo played on a team below my team," said Coach Harrison, "and sometimes his team wasn't playing in a tournament, and he was good enough to play up with me. Now, I didn't suggest he do that, he just never wanted to stop. The boy wanted to play all the time. We played 13 or 14 weeks in the summer, but if his team was off, he wanted to get with me, and he did for several tournaments. I knew he was an excellent player even before then, because I knew some of the daddies on the other team."

During Coach Harrison's 14-year-old season, when Stevo was 13, the team suffered several unfortunate injuries, losing a number of players from the field. At the same time, Stevo was unhappy with the coach's style on the 13's team he was playing with. Because of his prior experience, he knew he really wanted to be playing for Coach Harrison. Although it again meant playing up a year, Coach Harrison agreed to let Stevo take one of the open spots. After having proved his talent and his merit spot-playing in tournament play the previous two seasons, it turned out a good move for both Stevo and Coach Harrison.

"His desire to play was unmatched," Coach Harrison said. "When he came in, he was an influx of youthful excitement. When you get a kid like that, it's enjoyable to coach. With 11- and 12-year-olds, you can pretty much tell them what to do, and they listen. Once they reach 13, 14, they often think you're talking down to them. It's kind of like the young lion/old lion mentality. It's a hard group to coach, and after doing it for 40 years, I know what to expect. But Stevo was never like that. He never took criticism the wrong way; he always absorbed what I said."

As just another ongoing example of his on-the-field achievement, they named Stevo MVP for the game in July 2012 at the Elite 200 baseball showcase camp held at the University of Alabama.

"When he set his mind to do something, there was no lacking," Richard Sr., my father, said. "He's the one that would get right to it. He'd do it full blast, there was no halfway."

Throughout this period, I still coached some other players, and we worked a little one-on-one to improve skills his other coaches pointed out, but I was no longer head of his teams. Shelby's 16 now and we've moved in that same direction. Her teams have benefitted from me knowing more about how to deal with parents and various situations for playing time. Going in, I had a much better idea of how to handle all the competitive situations that arose so we could concentrate on the ballplayers.

In coaching the girls, I discovered there are some major differences between coaching girls and coaching boys. There's a different layer of skill set I wasn't prepared for and didn't expect. For example, there are elements to the maturity process I didn't know how to deal with. We had a big game coming up and our best pitcher was too out of sorts to play. Her mother asked me to have patience with her because it was her first time. All I could think about was, no it isn't. She's been our star pitcher for a while and has been in plenty of important games. It took several times before her mother finally got it through to me that our pitcher was experiencing her first period. Once I understood the language, I still struggled to understand how or why that should affect her game. These were issues I just never had with boys. Fortunately, by the time I got to the girls, I had already learned so much through coaching the boys that I could focus more on making these small but important adjustments.

Coaching a team of older girls as well as Shelby's team gave me time to learn from the older girls about these 'girl-specific' situations before I had to face them with Shelby's group. This was deliberate on my part because I wanted to be sure to give Shelby my best and I suspected there would be a few differences. I was grateful to have that chance as Shelby's group gained the benefit of a more informed coach, more sensitive to their particular concerns, which was also helpful in the process of moving the younger girls up to their competitive edge.

Knowing when to fall back was another lesson I learned from my son. I struggled to let go of the Memphis Tigers and coaching the boys' teams. Although Stevo had wanted to play football once he reached high school, the shoulder injury he sustained in middle school made him recognize the potential harm football could create in his baseball life. Rather than risk missing baseball, Stevo made a conscious decision to avoid playing football until his senior year. In doing so, he was showing me how to focus on my priorities, give up something in one area in order to maximize the benefit from another. As a football player in his senior year, Stevo found he still had some problems with the previously-injured shoulder. It would get stiff on him often, and some movements and stretches would cause him pain. Talking with the doctor about these complaints, the doctor's response was to point out how most of those movements weren't really doing anything to help his game and weren't needed. In other words, if it hurts, and it's not necessary, don't do it.

Of course, by then, he had already established and achieved more lofty goals thanks to his natural talent and charisma on and off the baseball diamond.

CHAPTER 7: GOOD ATHLETE

Most of Stevo's career thus far has been discussed in terms of extra-curricular youth sports in programs held outside of the school system. By middle school, Stevo was getting involved with his school teams, such as when he injured his shoulder playing basketball. But Stevo's aspirations as a youth sports player didn't stop at the school doors. He was equally determined to put his schools on the map through his sports. By the time he got to high school, he had decided it was time to put Munford High School on that map. From his freshman year, he played with the squad as the team's third baseman.

People really stood up and took notice when, as a sophomore, Stevo led the state in home runs with 13. He also was named District 13-3A MVP and All-Tournament Team that season. He hit two home runs in that championship game. That accomplishment, what many considered his breakout 2016 season, earned him a selection to the 11th annual POWER SHOWCASE All-American Team representing the state of Tennessee in the Underclassmen category. He also hit a few in the prestigious POWER SHOWCASE Home Run Derby.

"It just kind of caught fire last year with all those home runs," I told a local reporter back then. "They invited him

57

down in Miami along with the top 50 home run hitters across America."

He placed 15th, hitting one 468 feet.

"It was probably one of the longest ones I've ever hit," Stevo noted. "It was an awesome experience. I got to meet (major leaguer) Giancarlo Stanton down there. It was just awesome."

In taking on the challenge to take his school to state, note that Munford High School is the smallest of the schools in Tennessee's largest division, 6A. That put it at a distinct disadvantage in that it had the smallest pool of players competing against the state's most populated districts. The realities never daunted Stevo and, by the time he was done, they had gone all the way to state. Taking the school to the state championship and winning it all speaks volumes about the coaching, the training, and the talent they pulled together. It also says something about the subject of this book, Steven Kendrick, who stood out amongst the elite athletes all the way through graduation.

A friend since middle school, Brandon Baker, who everyone just called BB, and Stevo didn't start hanging out a lot until they were both in high school. It was BB's sophomore year and Stevo's freshman. BB described Stevo as outgoing, a very unselfish person, "which is probably the biggest thing."

"With baseball, he played with a lot of emotion and was really vocal, too," said BB. "He probably had the best chemistry with each player on the field. For instance, if he was catching, and the pitcher wasn't doing very well, he'd go talk to him. He always knew what to say to get 'em going. The way he handled himself on the field was enough to show how much of a leader he was, how much he cared, how much he wanted to win. He was that guy that changes momentum in the game real quick. If we were going slow, he was the one to change it."

Coach Scotty Yount was hired as head coach at Munford High just before the 2017 season, at the end of Stevo's sophomore season. His first season there, the coach had 13 seniors and three juniors, two of them being Nick Johnson, a left-handed power pitcher, and Stevo. This gave him a team loaded with seniors and two top talent juniors. He could put it all together and make a state championship run leading to Munford High School's first state appearance in 13 years. For Stevo, he was used to competitive play and playing for so many coaches by then. He was used to playing for whoever came up.

"Stevo was a junior when I came to Munford," Coach Yount said. "I lived in Bartlett then. When I took the job at Munford, I really didn't know anything about the team I was inheriting except that there was a kid that was going to the Home Run Derby in Miami during the fall. I streamed that game from my house. It was pretty cool. I kept thinking, 'He plays for me.' I also knew he led the state in home runs as a sophomore. I was excited about that, to have a player like that, but that was the only thing I knew of him."

"When he'd swing big and miss, he had this face, and he'd look over at the dugout as if to say, 'That was it—I should have hit that one. If I had that one it'd be going over the fence,'" BB said. "He always had that look. He had a big leg kick, so you knew he was about to swing hard."

I remember that look. Stevo called it "feeding the beast." That was his saying. You've got feed the beast, keep it coming, give him a play at the plate, feed him the ball to hit, give me the ball, that's how we're gonna win. That was him.

Pam remembered, "when he came up to the plate, he'd look back at the dugout to his teammates and rub his belly. Then, after he got a good hit, he'd get to the base and stand there and rub his belly. And they had another thing when they would shoot an arrow, like a bow and arrow."

One of the first times the team was on the field together that fall, Stevo was launching balls out left and right. Coach Yount had never coached a player that could do that.

"I was pretty impressed. Not only was he a hitter, but he could play any position on the field. I'd make him go get all the home run balls he'd hit out during batting practice, and he'd bring them back. Not everybody would go get them, but he would. Stevo always did the right thing. He played third base that first year, the year we went to the state tournament, and I'll tell you, I have never seen a better high school third baseman. He made plays that normal high school baseman do not make. It was his instincts, the way he could get his body in position to get rid of the ball quick and make plays. It was just something you can't teach—unbelievable player."

However, it was his tendency to want to swing big each time at bat that led Coach Yount to work with Stevo on swinging with more strategy. As usual, Stevo was coachable and seeking to improve.

"In terms of growing and developing, one of the biggest things was sometimes at his at-bats he would stay big in every single situation—the big swing at every single count," Coach Yount said. "I think he learned to back down a little off the big swings and put the ball in play. He knew how to handle the bat; he mastered it. For him, I was just making sure he was getting his foot down. When he went big, he had that leg kick, and when somebody was throwing with good velocity, he wouldn't get his foot down in time. When he had his foot down, he didn't miss the ball."

In games, if Coach thought Stevo was getting too big, especially if he thought the pitcher was throwing the ball with some good velocity, Coach would give him a fake-bunt-slash and he'd go right over the top with the ball.

"In the district tournament that junior year against Brighton (a 14-inning game), Cory Simmons got on in the 14th inning. I gave Stevo a fake-bunt-slash, and he hit a ball in the right-center gap and scored Cory all the way from first. We won it in the bottom of the 14th."

The two junior players on the team, Stevo and Nick Johnson, had been playing ball together since middle school and played like it in the run up to the state championship. After a while, the games blend together in memory, but one that still stands out was the Sectional game against Collierville that qualified them for the state tournament. Playing various positions, Stevo caught a no-hitter from Nick Johnson and recorded the final out in the field.

"When we beat Collierville in the sectional to go to the state tournament, the last out of the game was a three-hop ground ball to third base," said Coach Yount. "He bare-hands it, throws it to first, and we're going to state. The picture in the paper the next day was us dogpiling. I was on top of the dog pile with a big smile, and Stevo was right there with his back to the picture with 'Kendrick' on his back. That was a special one." They'd go on to qualify for the State Baseball Tournament in 2017.

That year was also the year Stevo and Nick played the quintessential perfect game held in Panama City, Florida. We headed south for a week-long college exposure event, jamming to Lil Troy's "Wanna Be a Baller." Stevo and Nick, who was riding with us, had never heard the song before, and it immediately became their anthem. Now every time I hear that song, I think of those boys just tearing it up. After that tournament, they played it everywhere they went.

We went down there, and they lit that tournament up. They had the best weekend ever down there. Stevo was busting the balls, making plays, and Nick pitched out of his head. The perfect game featured Stevo at third base and the lefty, of course, throwing to the plate. By then, both had been on scouts' radars for months and years. It was a no-hitter for Nick and what would be another perfectly played series of games for Stevo. Stevo played flawless defense with no errors, plus he finished among the top hitters during the week. What else could anyone expect at this point, particularly with Stevo? The boy had become a man—albeit still a young man—not just in sport, but in life.

Everyone who knew Stevo agrees that he always did the right thing, and he left several close friends behind that remember how his influence helped them. Like Nick, Stevo maintained a close relationship with Dustin "Dusty" Baker, another player he'd known since middle school while they were both still playing summer travel ball. By the time they reached high school, they were around each other most every day.

"When it came to the field, he really was a leader," Baker said. "Whether he was the catcher, playing third base, or on the mound, he always kept our team in the game. It was his intensity. Even off the field, he was always the guy I'd call to catch my pitches in the bullpen. I'd call him up and tell him I had to work on some stuff, so we'd go to the field. And nobody wants to catch the bullpen on a random weekday, but he was always the guy I'd call. I had another friend was also a pitcher, and he'd call Stevo, too. He was just catching the bullpen, but he was making himself better, too. He'd be blocking up balls, acting as if there was a runner going to second, working on other things you just wouldn't see out there unless you were in an actual practice. He just always had that intensity. He'd know how to get us in the zone, like if we had a bad arm angle or something, he'd walk out to us and say something like 'Just calm down, take a deep breath.'"

Every time Baker had a bad outing or just a bad inning, walking past Stevo warming up for his at bat, Stevo would tell him, "This one's for you. I'm getting us back in the game. I'm gonna hype us on up right here.'"

"Never failed," Baker said, "every single time, he'd do something that would get us back in the game."

Pam sometimes thought to herself, "Wow, he's so arrogant. But then I knew he was just so confident. Steven just had a way about him. He knew what he was doing, he knew what his outlook was. He lost track on how to get there sometimes, when he got overwhelmed or just burned out, but he always came back to fulfilling his dream."

BB also remembered Stevo's patience, on and off the field. With baseball, BB would "throw [a bad pitch] to him and he didn't care, he'd still hit it. He saw it as those bad throws were actually making him better; he'd swing even it was a pretty bad throw, he'd still make contact. Most of the games, I'd throw BP [Batting Practice] to him."

Stevo also inspired those several years younger than himself. One example happened right in front of Coach Yount as the Munford players were leaving for the state tournament. As the players and coaches were getting on the bus and backing out from the field, Coach Yount's wife, son Houston, and several others were there to see them off, waving goodbye. Houston was crying.

"He thought he should be with us," Coach Yount said. "I told the bus driver to stop and open the door. I jumped out and told him to come on (even though his mom was saying he didn't have any clothes), and here he comes, dead sprint—right past me and right to Stevo and Garrett Baugh on the bus. Stevo and Garrett spent a lot of time with him at practice every day. I remember coming home at night, and, if my kids had missed a game, the first question was whether we won. The second question was how Stevo did. He meant a lot to my kids."

The ultra-competitive environment that grew up around Stevo seemed to fuel his energy and talent, which went beyond baseball. He wanted to play football in high school, but he didn't go out for the team until his senior year. It was a scene at Munford High School during the summer preceding that year that Coach Barrlow will never forget.

"A memorable moment for me with Stevo was later when he was in high school, going into his senior year," Barrlow said. "We just ran into each other that summer. He was at the school, working out, and I asked him, 'Aren't you supposed to be playing baseball this summer?' He said, 'Coach, I'm playing football this year.' I asked him if he and his parents had talked about that. His parents and I had already talked about it some. Stevo had already had some offers to play baseball in college.

"Look, I love football. We live in the South and football is king. But football is dangerous, let's be honest. It's just part of that sport. So, I asked if he was sure, and he said, 'Coach, I'm playing football my senior year. I'm 18 and I don't need Mom and Dad to sign for permission."

As it turned out, though, Stevo had already talked with me about his feelings by then, and it was decided that he was going to play.

He told Coach Barrlow, "Dad knew he couldn't stop me from playing."

And he played. They went on to go 9-3 for the season, the best season that Munford High School had had in football.

"The core of that group were those boys surrounding Stevo since sixth grade that took me to a championship," Coach Barrlow recounts. "We had the best season that the school had recorded. That's him, as a linebacker, shoulder injury and all. One kid told me that if they got Stevo they'd be set on defense."

CHAPTER 8: GREAT SPORT

That innate leadership quality helped guide Stevo throughout his time on and off the field, season in, season out. It helped drive him to excel in his beloved sport, as did his unrivaled competitiveness, which administrators noticed during the school day as well.

"Steven was incredibly, incredibly competitive," Munford High School Principal Dr. Courtney Fee said. "As a principal, even in school, what you knew about that child was that he was a competitor. He was a competitor in the truest sense of the word. Even when he didn't love schoolwork, he would figure it out and do it to the best of his abilities, because that's what you did to compete. He wouldn't let anything get in his way, either. If people got fired up about something, Stevo didn't get fired up unnecessarily. He had his eye on the prize and nothing really got him sidetracked, which goes back to how competitive he was—he loved everything he did, from basketball to football to baseball, to life really."

At school, "Stevo would come in during 4th period, which was my off time," said Yount, "and he'd sit down, and it would just be the two of us. He'd watch hunting videos on YouTube on the big screen, and I'd ask him about hunting, because I'm not a big hunter. We had a lot of one-on-one talks. I trusted him enough as a player we'd go through these players—because I didn't know a lot of these players—and I'd say, 'Tell me about this hitter. Tell me about this pitcher.' He was just like another coach. He knew the game so well. This whole coach-player thing is about relationships. With Stevo, it wasn't all about baseball. I could go to Stevo and vent. He could come to me and vent. There was a trust there. And you don't have that with every player, like that. He was really larger than life."

For BB, it was fishing where he saw Stevo's patience and love of life most. Throughout high school, they were fishing partners, and Stevo taught BB everything he knew.

"He was unselfish in that way, too. We'd go out, and of course, when you do, you want to catch all the fish. But he didn't care, just so everybody caught fish, he was happy. He'd give me tips, he'd tell me what to do, what to throw. He was patient with me. Before, with others, you'd ask questions, and they'd get frustrated with you, but Stevo never did that. He always helped out, always made sure I knew what I was doing, made sure I caught them. I didn't know a single thing about fishing until I went out with him. Stevo taught me so much. Not just fishing or baseball or school, he was unselfish in every way. He was a leader in that way."

"Hunting, fishing, living, loving every day," Richard Sr. said. "You couldn't keep him out of the woods, couldn't keep him off the lake fishing."

Larger than life as a big brother, too.

"Stevo and Shelby were best friends," Pam said. "As is typical, they would argue and fight over the crazy, stupid stuff, but if they needed one another, they'd be there 100 percent. Stevo would always say, 'I don't want her around,' and then the first thing he'd say when he wanted to go do something was, 'Shelby, you want to come along with me?' He always looked out for her. In school, he got word on everything that was going on. Once, this kid was giving Shelby a hard time, and Stevo found that kid and said, 'Hey, that's my little sister, leave her alone.'

This playfulness between the siblings could get them in trouble at home, too. While the kids were still little and our family was living in the old house, the kids had a game room above the garage. It was a great place for them to play on rainy days without driving Pam and me crazy with pounding footsteps from above. At Stevo's funeral service, Shelby shared one of her favorite childhood stories from when she was 4 or 5.

Turtle had come over to spend the weekend with us and the three of them (Stevo, Turtle, and Shelby) were playing in the game room. I heard them running back and forth across the walkway that led to the house (and the upstairs bathroom), but I didn't think much of it. Turned out, they were practicing their sliding techniques for baseball, but the carpet in that room was not helping. So, they built an indoor water slide by filling 32 oz cups with water that they dumped directly into the carpet to make things easier. Except they were still sticking to the floor, so they added butter to the mix. They then proceeded to spend the rest of the afternoon slipping and sliding across the well-watered and buttered carpet.

It being the playroom, neither of us thought to check it until it was cleaning time the next weekend. When I opened the door, the smell just about knocked me over! We had to completely remodel the whole room. The carpet was ripped out, the floors sanded, and hardwood floors were put back in. Telling this story, Shelby had everyone listening chuckling along with her.

"Steven was always my idol," she said. "I always looked up to him. They call me little Stevo at school."

"He went to as many of her games as possible, and she went to way more of his. As soon as we could take Shelby out of the house after being born, she was at the baseball field for her brother's games. So she grew up in his world, which became her world."

This closeness did not go unnoticed by Munford High School Principal Dr. Courtney Fee.

"I just loved Shelby," Dr. Fee said. "I always thought we were going to have another little Stevo here at school. Shelby would come to pretty much all his games, and he was always the good big brother. From my viewpoint, if you could cookie-cutter how both Mom and Dad raised these two kids, you could sell it."

As much as a leader Stevo was in whatever sport he was playing, he was equally a leader in life.

"He and his family decided his freshman year that he would concentrate on baseball," Dr. Fee said. "Come his senior year, when they decided he would play football, he came to me to tell me he wanted to finish his high school career with the guys he had started his high school career with. That's the kind of kid he was. As a principal, I thought everything he was about was who he was to his family, to his teammates, to his coaches. He was always there for his teammates. It meant so much to him to be there for his teammates. That was defined him. Likewise, he was there for his family. He was the best big brother to his little sister, and he was out to be a good son. It was all about who he was to other people."

And other people included those less fortunate than him.

"He got involved with helping in the special education department," Dr. Fee said. "That's when he started thinking about what he would like to do, which was lining up with teaching. He had done a camp with the little kids, and these kids were just hanging off him. And that's how he was. The kids loved him, adults loved him, everybody loved him. He was just the greatest kid to be around. It was his senior year or the summer after his senior year, and I remember asking him, 'You ever think about teaching?' He said, 'You know Miss Fee, I've been thinking about it lately.'"

Pam concurs: "He expressed an interest in teaching when he got older. What was amazing to me was that Munford went through a couple of baseball coaches during his time there before Coach Yount came, and he loved Coach Yount. He said soon afterwards that he wanted to be a coach, coming back to Munford High after college to be a teacher-coach. And he said, 'I'm not going to be just the assistant coach, I'm going to be THE coach.' I laughed and told him, 'I'm sure your day will come.'"

Stevo would help with the special ed kids one period per day during his junior year.

"We have student assistants help in that department, and we have a couple of coaches that are part-time special ed teachers," Dr. Fee explained. "It was about 90 minutes a day that these kids assisted the coaches. The young men who are special ed students have severe and/or profound needs (they may not be verbal, they may be in a wheelchair, have cerebral palsy, developmentally delayed), and they can be of good size, strong kids, so it was good to have someone of Stevo's size there to help walk them and feed them or be a buddy at lunch. These student assistants just joke with them and cut up, just treat them like normal kids. That experience teaches compassion.

"Then, at camp with all the little kids, Stevo was Mr. Popular. They absolutely loved him."

Stevo learned valuable life lessons at home, but good coaches constantly reinforced those values.

"Talking to Stevo and his teammates collectively, my thing was with them was I don't never want to pick up the newspaper and read that you have violated the things we talked about," Coach Barlow said. "Those things were love of self and others, respect of law, respect of your country. We used to discuss those things all the time before practice, not just the player we want to be, but the person we want to be, which is more important.

"My life is great, but the best four years were here when I coached middle school basketball. I used to tell them they don't want to look back and have regrets—leave it on the court, leave it on the field, leave it on the diamond, leave it on the mat, in the classroom. You don't want to look back and think, I wish I would have studied a little harder. You leave everything you've got right there, so you'll have some exceptional experiences and you know you gave it 100 percent."

Stevo took Coach Barrlow's advice to heart. Surveying Stevo's life, it's clear that he gave even more than 100 percent, packing as much of life as a day may permit, and leaving a legacy being lived out today and for years to come in those he affected.

In practice, he taught his teammates to do what it takes to win.

"If he had to put somebody in the wall, that's what he'd do, within the context and rules of the sport," Coach Barrlow recalled. "That's Stevo. He was a starter beginning as a 6th grader. I've only had Stevo and another guy in that group that's done that for me. All that rubs off. When you see a guy with major minutes diving after a loose ball, if I'm that guy coming off the bench, I know what I need to do. He didn't have to say what needed to happen—it was action."

And this action led to an offer to play college ball. Colleges wanted Stevo obviously for his big bat, but also for his versatile play on the field. With team success and individual numbers, we received offers from across Tennessee and even as far as South Carolina. But the ideal fit for Stevo in his heart was close to home.

Almost to the date when Stevo took part in the home run showcase in Florida while with the Cougars, he was signing his letter of intent to join the Southwest Tennessee CC baseball program. Flanked by myself and Pam, with Shelby and Stevo's coaches in the wings, Stevo signed on January 26, 2018.

When an interviewer with The Munford Star asked about where he got his baseball knowledge, Stevo remembered our early days. He told the interviewer, "Me and my dad started in my garage. Weekends, late nights, all the time, just me and him hitting all along until Coach Griggs, my head coach on the Memphis Tigers, coaching me more on my swing. It kind of all built from there. It kinda just caught fire.

"Baseball helped me realize that you're only as good as your weakest player," Stevo told the reporter. "Every teammate needs everyone else. Moving from pitcher to position player, we had to have a lot of guys pitch. We had to go deep into our rotation because we're the smallest school in our league. Everybody getting their job done showed me you have to be able to play multiple positions. The signing takes a lot of weight off my shoulders — hoping people are looking at you or hoping people will recruit you. But with that weight lifted, I can just have fun and play baseball with my friends my senior year."

Stevo was listed as first base/designated hitter at 5'9" and 215 lbs. Nick Johnson, the talented pitcher and Stevo's childhood friend, signed on the same day as Stevo. He was also going to Southwest.

Do Skunks Swim?

CHAPTER 9: THE FINAL INNING

Things were going well for Stevo and his friends. They finished their senior year in style and graduated. Steven and Nick had also finished with baseball scholarships. It was November 13, 2018, when tragedy struck the group again. Stevo's teammate and classmate, Chase Suggs, another baseball standout, died in an ATV accident in Drummonds, Tennessee.

Suggs played at Brighton High before transferring to Munford for his senior year, but he and Stevo had played on the same teams in tournament play since middle school.

"Chase was infectious," Coach Yount told the Covington Leader. "He had the ability to make everyone around him smile. Chase was kind, respectful, and always took time for others. My two boys loved Chase because he always played catch with them and always asked about their days at school. Chase had a baseball player mentality. He overcame some adversity and really made a positive impact here at Munford his senior year. Personally, Chase and I really created a tight bond."

Even after graduation, Suggs had a habit of hanging around the baseball team through the spring. Yount told the Covington Leader the two had texted often, Suggs came to visit him and the rest of the guys regularly.

"I will miss him dearly," Yount said.

Stevo had been with Suggs the day he died. He planned to be out riding ATVs with him. The two had been hanging out with several friends before going out riding. Stevo's machine was broken at the time. He tried to convince Suggs to stay at the house with him and the rest of their friends, but the guys went out, anyway. According to reports, Suggs died at approximately 8 p.m. when the Honda ATV he was driving went off Highway 59 West on a curve and struck a utility pole. According to the Tennessee Highway Patrol, there were no other vehicles involved, and he was the only person on the ATV. Suggs was only 19 years old.

They held a balloon release memorial ceremony later at the Mississippi River attended by friends, family, and ex-teammates. I took Stevo and his girlfriend, Julie, to the funeral. It crushed me to see Suggs' parents in their grief. Parents are not meant to bury their children. I remember telling Stevo at the time how careful he needed to be, warning him once again about the dangers of taking reckless risks. I didn't think I could survive it. Stevo assured me he understood everything I'd been trying to teach him about growing up and the potential consequences that could happen. I left the funeral feeling better that he understood everything that was happening and could make mature, responsible decisions. His practicality and ability to follow through gave me a false sense of security that my son would be all right.

Coach Yount was unfortunately somewhat familiar with losing an athlete at a young age. In 2002, Hayes Kent, a 16-year-old Bolton High School player, died in a car accident. The accident happened before Yount became the coach there, but it still affected him. He helped organized a basketball tournament to raise funds for a scholarship in Kent's honor. With the loss of Suggs, Yount again took action, this time approaching Jack and Brooke Suggs with another scholarship, this time in their son's name. The Chase Suggs scholarship is awarded to two Munford High senior baseball players each year.

It had been a long, trophy-gathering span of time since Stevo played noodle ball back in Delaware. Soon he would showcase his skills at USA Stadium. This field is where the U.S. Olympic teams come to train, and what Stevo would call his home field for college exposure ball. He had made it. He had survived childhood and was on his way out into the world—a young man on the verge of amazing things. Instead, in the home-team locker room, Stevo's locker remains reverently untouched, as do his two pairs of cleats, dirt still caked on them. These have become sacred spaces.

Just a few months later, on Saturday, January 26, 2019, Stevo was busy from even before sunrise. The plan was for us to go duck hunting, but our boat wasn't usable, so it made sense for Stevo to go with his friends instead. The place we went ended up being frozen over and didn't have any birds, so it worked out better for Stevo, anyway.

Among the friends that went hunting with Stevo that day was his new Southwest Tennessee teammate Nicholson Sparks. Nick was a new transplant to the area. He was a pitcher, having attended McNairy Central High School (Tennessee) and played summer ball with Henry County. They had much better luck than we did. Stevo and Nick bagged their two-man limit before leaving for baseball practice. After they left, the others who stayed behind apparently got another 20 birds.

After baseball practice, Stevo and his girlfriend Julie had plans to get tattoos and then attend a party some of their mutual friends were throwing. Stevo was planning to get a tattoo in commemoration of a beloved aunt, Pam's sister, who recently passed away. But when they stopped back at home for Stevo to change, he told Julie he'd rather stay home and catch up on his rest. There was only one more day left of duck-hunting season, and he knew he'd be up early again the following day. No tattoo, no party.

As always, Stevo pre-packed his hunting bag, decoys ready, before turning in for the night.

That false sense of security kicked in for me again. Here was my son, choosing to stay home instead of going to a party because he was tired and planned to get up early in the morning for more hunting.

They planned to meet at Nick's apartment that morning, but numerous text and phone messages prove Stevo had a hard time waking Nick up for the trip to St. Francis County, Arkansas, near the town of Colt, about 80 miles away. It had even been necessary for Stevo to call a mutual friend, Gentry, who lived in the same complex, to let Steven in through the main gate. Gentry remembered buzzing Stevo through and wishing him luck on the duck hunting for that morning. Nick had clearly not gotten enough sleep the night before. He'd been out with friends until around 2:30 am which would have him home by 3. Stevo was waking him up at 4:30. Still, the boys took Nick's new F-150 instead of Stevo's truck, meaning Nick was driving.

It haunted me that maybe they'd taken Nick's truck because Stevo didn't have the gas money, but I checked. Stevo's truck still had three-quarters of a tank of gas in it, plus he had $100 in an account from me and more money in an account from his mom. Gas money was not the issue. Despite the new vehicle, the two never reached their destination.

According to the Arkansas State Police report, the truck left the road just outside of Colt at about 6 a.m., running into a ditch and striking a driveway before coming to a stop. There appeared to be no brake marks on the street or in the grass on the shoulder of the road, indicating the truck was going full speed when it hit the ditch. Stevo was ejected almost immediately upon impact, straight through the truck's closed sunroof. Nick followed soon thereafter. Nick landed in mud, which helped save his life. Stevo, however, was killed in the process of being thrown from the truck.

Stevo would have turned 20 within two weeks. To the day, as newspaper reports noted, it was exactly 85 days since Chase Suggs had passed, the time for a regular season of baseball. It was also exactly one year since Stevo signed on to play for Southwest.

"They informed me of Stevo's accident," Dr. Fee said, "and then someone told me that his and Shelby's mom was not in town, that she was in California, and no one knew if she knew yet. As a principal, one of your first thoughts is where I needed to be, and I knew somebody needed to be with Shelby. We had just dealt with the passing of Chase Suggs, and at first, you just don't believe it. But you have to believe it, and we knew we had to get people through it. I texted Shelby's mom and asked her where she wanted me to be. My first thought was Shelby, because I knew how close she and her big brother were. I have a big brother, and we're close, too. I knew how important it was."

In California for work on that day, Pam was preparing for the start of a racing event as a racing promoter. She had just walked out of a racer's trailer when someone asked how her day was going.

"I'm having a fabulous day," Pam said. "Then my phone rang, and it was Shelby. She didn't know about Steven at the time either, so we're just talking about the upcoming day. I got off the phone with her, and one of the girls who worked with me walked up to me and asked if I had heard from anyone back home. She could tell from my eyes that there was something I didn't know. She asked if anyone had talked to me about Steven, and when I asked her what it was, she couldn't verbalize what had happened. I called Kendrick, but he didn't know anything either. That was around 1 p.m. back home. Finally, by word of mouth, another coworker told me Steven was in an accident. As soon as she said that, I knew it was tragic."

Pam's boss bought her an airline ticket to fly back immediately. Flights were being cancelled and delayed, but as she said, "by the grace of God, I got back later that night around midnight."

I was in town, at work, but I didn't get word until hours later, in the early afternoon, from one of my coworkers.

As I mentioned earlier, the night before we buried my boy, I didn't know how to handle it. We always packed up the night before to go on hunting trips, so maybe that was why packing his backpack came to me. We had matching backpacks. I was looking at putting my boy to rest; he was leaving, and so in the back of my brain, I thought I had to pack him up one more time. So, I packed him up for a trip. I gave him water, Gatorade, his favorite Pringles, you name it, he had it in his bag—there's nothing my boy's lacking.

When I finished packing, I went into his room and sat in his chair, looking around and asking, 'Bud, what else do you need?' At the same time, I was saying, 'What happened, man, what went wrong? Why is this happening?'

It came to me he needed a book to read. I looked at his bookcase, with all the titles facing out, and one book stood out—the author Nicholas Sparks' name stared out at me. I pulled that book out, and it caught me. It was as if, once I asked what went wrong, my boy answered and directed me to that book, to let me know about Sparks. I was in shock, overwhelmed. In that moment, I felt like my boy told me what happened and what went wrong.

His mother now has that book; I couldn't keep it in the house.

As far as Sparks goes, we have all had mixed feelings.

Pam said, "I've wondered about how Stevo would want me to feel, how to approach this kid. In my heart, at the time just after the wreck, I felt like Stevo wouldn't want to see another life taken, meaning he has his entire life ahead of him to remember this; he'll always have this burden on his heart, and somehow he has to move on with his life. That's how I truly felt, until I wondered so much about who this kid was, about how things happened, and what had truly happened."

When the toxicology report was finally released, police notified us that Nick was high on marijuana at the time of the crash. They issued a warrant for his arrest on charges of negligent homicide, Class B felony. Later, they offered Nick a plea deal and he pled guilty to negligent homicide, Class C misdemeanor, and the sentence was reduced accordingly.

"My perspective changed to almost an anger," Pam continued, "particularly after finding out that the attorneys came to some sort of settlement, where the charges were so much less. I think about that and wonder if he's going to realize what he did. As far as we can all see, there doesn't seem to be any remorse. It seems he should be going to drug rehab or not have his license for a while. He needed to learn a lesson from this, build from it, and take something away from it. I don't know that that's happened, given how the attorneys negotiated and lessened the charge and penalty. In the court, it didn't seem my son's life was valued, and that hurts.

"I think the anger has taken away how I initially felt. I have to find a way to forgive, although I'll never forget."

While we've both struggled with our feelings about Sparks, I glean some comfort from the fact that Stevo passed instantly. According to police reports at the scene of the accident, and later confirmed, Stevo had been asleep when the truck left the road and was likely only awake a second or two as the vehicle bounced and rolled, until the instant he was ejected through the closed sunroof. The fact that he was only awake for a moment gave me a little breathing room through the suffocating shock and grief that followed.

Thousands turned out for the funeral. The only thing that brought me comfort was the thought that, on the day of his accident, my son was living his life.

As I was cleaning up after the college teammates left following the funeral, it was about 2 am and I still had the small card Stevo had given me when I'd left the airport for my first commute, way back when he was two years old in my pocket. I was standing alone in my kitchen, feeling completely alone, and broke down. Into the silence, the recorded voice of my infant son told me, I love you, Daddy. It happened three more times through that first night. This has never happened in the more than 20 years I've had this card near me. It hasn't happened since that night. But that night, it was the sign I needed that my son was still with me, and always will be.

The light was left on in Stevo's room that early morning after he had left to go hunting. It was something we often argued about—remembering to switch the lights off, as parents and children do. The first thought I had when I saw the light shining into the hallway from under his door that morning was how we'd have to have a talk later, again. On this day, however, and for days and months and years to come, the light will stay on 24/7. It is now a tribute to the light that Stevo gave the world.

Moments and hours after life's breath left Stevo, the air was sucked out of Tipton County as news got out.

CHAPTER 10: THE LAST CALL

Stevo wasn't just a hero to his family, he was a hero to the entire community. As news of his death spread, the world seemed to draw in, and we started hearing more and more about what Stevo meant to others.

"His passing was tough, and it's still tough," Coach Barrlow said. "I told my mom that my dream was that they would bury me—all my players. Of course, I can't even imagine his father and mother. When they give them to you to coach and to nurture, they trust you to instill the same values as they have at home. I've lost two players now, an older player that passed, and I remember Chase, too. It's been tough. As for the community itself, it's been very difficult of course. Young people taken in the prime of their lives."

The words are clearly hard to find, hard to articulate. How can you capture the overwhelming and unquantifiable loss of such promising young men? How does one cope with the loss of the light they brought?

Coach Barrlow has embraced the knowledge of never knowing how long someone will stay in your life. He now advises everyone to tell people how you feel at every opportunity.

"Don't take things for granted so often," he said. "Be mindful and be thankful that you had a short time in their lives, especially from my perspective, because playing sports and coaching sports, there are conversations that we have had that no one knows about. But it was fun, fond memories."

Stevo's locker at Southwest remained as it was the last time he was in the locker room for two seasons. They did this to honor and remember him. In addition, "SK11," Stevo's number, was painted on the infield turf at USA Stadium Southwest, on either side of the pitching lane, and remained there through the 2021 season.

"As time goes by, it really settles in—why him?" Dr. Fee said. "He was such a great kid. I know it's not for me to ask why. I think that's such a big reason we want Mr. Kendrick to be a part of us at school. It's our way of really keeping Stevo's memory alive. And when I say alive, it's not just something that's going to stand there and remind of us of him. Instead, this is the way for us to do what we know that child would do if he were alive today. You can't just walk away from his memory; he was that type of kid."

"The Kendricks are going through what I went through with the passing of my wife," Michael Robinson said. It has been nine years since his wife was shot and killed at that post office, but the pain remains. "You learn how to deal with it on a daily basis. My wife loved Steven, loved the Kendricks."

"Every other morning or so Alabama's song 'Angels Among Us' will pop up, and that was Stevo's song, at least to me," Principal Fee said. "He was our man. I told his mom that, as principal, as a school leader, I asked myself 'If you know these are the last four years of this child's life, are you leading a school that you would be proud to say that these were the last four years of this child's life?' He made me not want to disappoint him as his school's principal. Even in his death, you think you must make sure that this is a kid you don't forget, because there is so much you learned from him, including the fact that these four years are very important to children. It could be their last four."

During Stevo's junior year, Stevo clicked with an assistant coach, Jeremy Finney, who was also a police officer. This coach had played college baseball, and Stevo respected him a great deal, growing close to him. Out of mutual respect, Coach Finney wrote this poem after Stevo's death to honor him:

Sliding Into Home
Some say baseball is just a game.
But to us Life and Baseball are just the same.
Whether it's balls and strikes or Highs and Lows,
We are taught to get back up after each blow.
You were a scrappy kid with a big swing.
A player with all the tools, your jersey never clean.
I was a police officer looking for a change of pace.
I knew helping at Munford High was just the place.
You wanted the ball in your hand on the biggest stage,
Always one of the first ones to arrive at the cage.
No matter the cost, you always paid your dues.
You always wanted to know the latest police news.
You spoke of hunting and your little sister Shelby.
But you had no idea how much you helped me.
You showed me how to compete and how to play.
You put in time with my son each and every day.
You showed me a bulldog mentality with every inning
you'd hurl.

You showed me off the field there are still good people
in this world.
You were a ballplayer, hunter, Brother, and a son,
But to me you were Second to None.
On the diamond we were at peace and never alone.
Send us a picture of you in Heaven,
Sliding into Home.

Stevo's Aunt RaRa, Pam's sister, went to every one of Stevo's early games she could when they still lived in Dover. I'm not sure if she ever missed one. Once we moved to Memphis, it was harder for her to come, but she traveled as often as she could to watch him play and wrote in her journal about how fast the time flew from little boy to getting his driver's license, to graduating high school. The last time she saw Stevo alive was on her way home from a vacation, when they stopped in Memphis to see Pam. Stevo and some of his friends came by from college to say hello.

"They played a game called Spoons, and I didn't play. Oh, how I wished I played. I had no idea that would be the last time I saw him. I want people to know he was a great young man. What you saw is what you got."

"I'd tell people, there he goes, he's my hero," Richard Sr. said. "Turns out he was a lot of people's hero. The main thing I tried to teach him was to tell the truth. I told him I wouldn't lie to him, just don't lie to me. That way we wouldn't ever have a disagreement about anything. I told his dad the same thing growing up."

It was as they fished that Richard Sr. passed along his lifetime of wisdom to his grandson.

"I had big plans for Steven," Richard Sr. said. "I wanted him to get married and not get divorced. He would have been the first one, the first Kendrick, to get married and not divorced. Sometimes I think you're not a Kendrick if you've not been divorced two or three times. That was my dream for him—to get married and stay married. He and I were out fishing, and I told him if he could just break this spell of divorce. That and living a sober life.

"We come from a long line of alcoholics, my daddy included, and I wanted to break that curse with my son. I think that's come along well, because he's not out at the bars chasing women like I did. In fact, as far as taking care of business and life, he does that better than any Kendrick there was. I was so proud of him for getting his degree, turning out like he has. And there's no way I could be any prouder I was of Stevo. He did more in 18 years than most people do in 80. He did a lot of stuff and been to a lot of places."

My dad also wrote a few poems in Stevo's honor, remembering how his grandson changed his perspective of the world:

Where did Stevo go?
Where did Stevo go?
I saw him jump across the clouds. He had his hat and glove on. He must've been going to the mound.
I guess the Lord called him in to pitch, as the clouds slowly came together.
I called out his name again, knowing he's gone forever.

-- Richard Kendrick Sr.

The kid went down to Miami, where the Florida Marlins play.
Big jump for a young kid, who was feeling real nervous and all.
His dad flew down from Memphis, and the ball went over the wall.

-- Richard Kendrick Sr.

Seems like I see those ones everywhere I go.
They're on the TV, they're on the cash register, they're
on the radio.
The number 11 will always make me smile... and cry.
That's the way it will be until the day I die.
SK11: Live Love Dream

-- Richard Kendrick Sr.

The death of my son is, by far, the hardest thing I will ever go through in my life, but from the end of 2018 to the start of 2020 was an especially hard time as we lost more than just Stevo. It started with Chase, then Stevo. My old boss died from the effects of cancer just two weeks after I lost my boy. Then, a little girl I'd coached and one of Shelby's friends died on March 5, 2019, at age 15.

Megan Cox had a rare stomach disorder, so they fed her with a tube and through IV for about two years prior to her death, but it wasn't enough. The poor child ended up starving to death despite all the medical community could do for her. I couldn't let Shelby go with me to that funeral. I was too afraid to take her. Not six months prior, I'd taken Stevo to his old teammate's funeral and followed that up by carrying my own son in his. It was too soon, too eerily similar. I needed to interrupt the pattern, so I went to that funeral alone.

As if losing one supportive boss wasn't enough, Richard Curry, the boss that had supported me through our losses, died on November 5, 2019, followed just more than a week later by a mentor to my son and me, Mike Loyd. He blew the final duck call at Stevo's funeral because he'd been the man who first introduced us to the sport. Because of him, I have many wonderful memories of spending time with my son off the ball field.

Pam and I never realized, but when you look at who the pallbearers were at my son's funeral, they were a mix of age and race. Stevo didn't discriminate, he didn't judge. His friends were from all over. Stevo attacked hunting and fishing like he attacked the ball. He just ate it up. As a little boy, when I told him he couldn't hunt or fish, that was the end of the world! A lot of times it was because I had to work, and I was saving my vacation time so I could do ball. But Mike always encouraged me to keep at it and take my boy hunting. I am so grateful for Mike, who gave me this gift of time with my son and want to honor him for it. We lost Mike the same year we lost Stevo.

Mike Loyd

April 5, 1970 – Nov. 16, 2019

To finish out the tragic year, I received a call in early 2020, informing me that another one of my son's teammates had a sister that passed away at just 22 on New Year's Eve. The family had been close to ours and so helpful through everything we'd been through. It was heartbreaking to hear this news.

Stevo's burial site seemed divinely reserved for my son, just across the street from his hometown ball field. As you drive on the paved road that leads to Munford High School's entrance, Centennial Ballpark is on the left with the school itself just beyond the field. Immediately across the road from center field is the burial site, his memorial marker prominent. We placed him with his feet nearest the rise to the road, so he could see every game played from now on. My boy will always be under the lights.

CHAPTER 11: LIVE, LOVE DREAM

I'm not proud of it, but I admit, I spent New Year's Eve trying to drink 2019 away. To make the evening special, I headed to a rooftop bar at a high-end hotel in downtown Memphis with a clear mission to drink the year away. To make sure things went smoothly, I even paid the bartender up front and tipped $100 for an open bar to keep the drinks coming. Making sure I didn't have to wait for the next drink, I tipped an extra $10-$20 every third drink or so. It took me three days to recover.

You might remember I'd stopped drinking completely the moment Stevo came into my life. For almost 20 years, I hadn't had more than one drink at any setting and only on rare occasions. Many of those years passed without me touching any alcohol at all. But the thought of starting a new year without my son in it was something I didn't want to face and couldn't comprehend. The bottle won that night as I searched for my son at the bottom of a glass, but I soon realized I couldn't find him in that place. Drinking didn't help lessen the pain. It didn't stop time or change the realization of how my life was going to be. From that moment forward, I would never be the same person again.

I felt lost and adrift without my son to guide me. I'd prepared to release Stevo as he finished his college years, spent time with Julie, and went off to the rest of his life, but

I'd never considered releasing him to death. I remember thinking a father has nothing left without his son. There was nowhere for me to grow without him. It had always been Stevo showing me the way. As I wrote at the beginning of this book, one of the first things that came up for me in therapy following Seven's death was the realization that he was my anchor and my rudder from the moment he came into my life. I had no idea how to chart my course without him, yet, at the same time, I was compelled to keep moving forward.

Part of the difficulty here was Stevo was my true mini-me. I'd taught him everything I knew and he shared my passions for everything. From sports like football, baseball, coaching, and competition to our love for the outdoors with hunting and fishing. We even shared a love for spaghetti. From the very beginning, Stevo was my baby. Then he grew into my little man, my son, and my best friend. Every passion I had, I shared with my son, so moving forward was especially difficult. Everything I could think to do, even down to watching a football game, is painful to me now. Being in the Timber Hole or on the lake is painful because I don't have him with me. Trying to discover new things to be interested in is also difficult because each new passion I find, the first thing I want to do is share it with him.

Shortly after laying Steven to rest, all these emotions were washing over me, leaving me feeling completely lost and confused. I had a dream where these feelings were following me. In the dream, I found myself at a party where there was a lot of noise. People were milling about, all of them talking, all at the same time, but none of their words made sense. I couldn't figure out where I was, why I was there, what I was supposed to be doing, and couldn't understand any of the people around me for a clue. I was starting to panic when I felt myself lifting, my feet leaving the floor. I looked to my left and saw a man I knew, but I didn't know who he was. He had my left arm around his shoulders and was carrying my weight, but I was evenly balanced. I looked to my right and saw my son, Stevo, supporting me in the same way on that side. I knew Stevo was gone and couldn't believe he was there next to me.

"Are you seeing this?" I asked the man to my left.

The man nodded his head yes.

I heard a short laugh from the other side and turned to look at my beautiful son again.

Sadness came into his eyes as he looked back at me. "I'm sorry, Dad. I'm just out of time."

With that, both Stevo and the other man disappeared, leaving me floating in sleep.

When I woke up and was getting ready for work, I realized I still felt all the loss, pain, confusion, and sorrow, but something had changed. None of those other emotions had reduced in the slightest, but I didn't feel so alone anymore. I knew my son was still with me.

At first, I thought that other man must have been Jesus, but after thinking about it, I believe it was probably my baby brother, Stephen. He died when he was an infant, which is why I knew him but didn't know him. I'd never met him as a man.

It was a powerful dream that I continued to feel for a long time. It continues to remind me I was never alone. Now, when I try to discover new activities to involve myself with, I remind myself of this. Stevo is always with me, so in moving forward, in discovering these new things, I am bringing him with me, letting him see these things through my eyes. I talk to him continually and often.

My grief for Steven has been a never-ending roller coaster of emotion. It's like being dropped into a bottomless pit in the beginning. Everything is coming at you so fast, and nothing can be done. Everything, every step, seems for nothing. The pain is unbearable. It's indescribable, something no one can or has been able to comprehend except those that face the nightmare. Nightmare isn't even an accurate term because you can wake up from a nightmare. Our minds are not properly wired for facing this type of death. We're programed to understand a specific order of things and how life proceeds. As parents raise their children, the mindset is that this little person will someday be the person putting me to rest. We work and build everything toward their ability to succeed us. When a parent finds themselves with a child's loss, the whole process of life and building toward one's goals becomes a chaotic mess. Questions of 'why' and 'what was all this for' arise. Not just questions of why did I lose my child, but why anything? What am I doing and for who?

Yes, I have a daughter who has provided me with the strength needed to semi-answer some of these questions, but something still seems lost, the motivational drive seems gone. I started looking for anything that could be a sign of what I should do now. These became things such as a cardinal in the yard every day, all year long; a butterfly at one of Shelby's games at a moment of extreme sadness; one-and-one of everything—two mallards, two geese with their necks stretched tall – always seem to be close; every purchase and every number seems to correlate back to 11. The number 11, Stevo's number, is everywhere.

I had a second dream not too much later, this one much shorter but no less profound. Just as I was starting to doubt my way again, I dream-woke in the passenger seat of Stevo's truck. He was driving and laughing. He was so happy as he looked back at me. He smiled extra wide, rubbing his stomach like we used to do after a particularly filling meal. I don't remember if he actually said the words or if I just heard them in my mind, the meaning that look between us had always meant.

"I'm good, Dad. I'm still eating good and doing all right."

It was a more comical way of Stevo letting me know I wasn't alone. He is always going to be with me.

It is natural at these times of extreme loss and sadness; I believe some start questioning God and actually even become furious with God. I've chosen to believe that God knows my pain. Even He couldn't bear the loss of his own son Jesus for more than three days. Although I found some comfort in church, I needed more than what Sundays could give me. I started attending a men's group held at Millington Baptist Church on Wednesday nights called Kingdom Man. The class had just started up when I needed that extra help, so it seemed like a fit made just for me. Within the group, we talk about what a Kingdom Man is and what's needed for a Kingdom Man to serve God. Through this group and my regular worship, I found my peace with the Lord.

No matter what religious perspective you come from, they all talk about an afterlife, that you keep on going after death. That's what keeps me going today, knowing that I'll see him again. In the military, they tell you you woke up that day. That simple fact is enough to get you through that day. You woke up today is unofficial code for "you have the opportunity/ responsibility/ obligation to live today, to make a difference." You take the same directive to keep stepping forward the next day, and the day after that. Each day brings you that much closer to completing your mission. I wake up each morning knowing I'm one day closer to seeing Stevo again. I carry this faith each day. I know I'm not getting any younger and each sunrise brings me and my son closer to being in each other's arms again. And when I see him, I want him to know I didn't let him down. I fulfilled his expectations for me; I honored his memory, and I continued to grow no matter how much it hurts.

In talking with other parents who have suffered these losses and in my own situation, I've come to discover a common phenomenon. Other people don't know how to talk to us. They seem afraid to hurt us and, instead, won't approach us. They avoid talking to us about our lost child, whisper in the past tense when it's absolutely necessary to bring up the subject, and generally try to avoid the topic of children altogether.

If I could stand on a stage to speak on behalf of all parents who have lost a child, I would tell the world to speak up. Talk to us about our children. Give us a space to remember them, share their stories, celebrate their lives, and yes, grieve them when we need to. What I don't think most people realize is that our children are not past tense for us. They are always here with us, in our hearts and minds. We want to talk about them. More often than not, talking about our children makes us happy and helps us stay focused on living forward.

Pam is the one who remembered the "soundbite" moment that helped me move forward after my son's death. As a high school junior in 2017, Stevo's friend Sarah talked him into participating in the Mr. MHS pageant for a fundraiser. As part of the competition, each participant had to go up to the microphone, say their name, and tell the audience something about themselves. Stevo won that year because when he walked to the front of that stage, he told the crowd, "I'm Steven Kendrick and I will put Munford High School on the map." Mic drop. He walked off the stage.

I knew that for Stevo, putting Munford on the map meant more than just what he could do with his swing. His wish was for me to do for Shelby in her softball aspirations what I'd done for him. It's clearer than ever that Stevo was wise beyond his years, a rare quality. He'd always taught me how to do things. He showed me my potential. I have my A&P (Airframe and/or Powerplant) license that allows me to work on airplanes, something I never would have pursued if it hadn't been for my boy. I didn't start training for it until Pam was pregnant. He was born in '99 and I got hired on at FedEx in 2001 because I got my A&P license in 2000. That allowed me to earn more, to provide better, and to give more. Then, when he took to baseball, we ran with it.

Fast forward six months after the funeral, and a new vision took concrete shape in the form of Stevo's wish to put Munford on the map, initially to coach Shelby and morphing into taking it all the way. This is the most palpable way Stevo continues to live in my heart and through my actions. Shelby has picked up her brother's mantle, starting varsity as a freshman, just like her brother did in high school and was about to do, starting on the A team in college.

"Their closeness was amazing, as close as a brother and sister could be," Pam said of the brother-sister relationship. "Shelby's still struggling with the fact that she's lost her best friend. A big part of her heart is ripped out."

Playing through the pain just like her brother did, on the weekend of March 23-24, 2019, Shelby won her first softball tournament since the accident—an amazing feat, considering all that we had been through. She played well in the game, played third base, just like Stevo. She started third base in high school as a freshman, just like Stevo, most definitely following in his footsteps. Playing at that level says a lot about young Shelby, even as Stevo continues to show me a way.

At the center of my drive was always Stevo, who, with plenty of hard work, dedication, and focus, rose to the top of his favorite game. Even as I continue to wrestle with the why of Stevo's passing, the drive we shared for Shelby, for the game, and for our town lives on.

The goal now is to take the softball program to the state championship and win it, to put Munford on the map as Stevo had wanted us to do. We want to make Munford something to be feared on anyone's schedule.

Toward increasing Munford's reputation, plans are also underway to build a state-of-art training facility. We'll call it the SK11 Training Facility. We hope to have that underway by 2022. I'll be doing everything I can to make that happen until it does.

"When Kendrick first came to us, I told him, 'if you do this, it will be some of the most purposeful living you will ever do,'" Dr. Fee said. "But only if he could handle it. Some people can't handle it emotionally, but he is. He's doing what I can totally see Stevo doing. Kendrick is obviously very talented and we're so happy he's here. I can see that he's wanting Stevo to be proud of who he is, of what he's doing. He's looking for that purposeful living every day. And Stevo was like that. He didn't do anything half-fail. He was going to live life to the fullest."

The training facility will keep Stevo's memory alive for generations, as will an annual scholarship recognizing the spirit of not only his play on the field but his generosity and leadership that brands his legacy. The scholarship is called the Gamechanger Award and will be given to the student-athlete who best exemplifies the type of game-changing leadership and sportsmanship that made Stevo stand out.

Breaking it down through the years and looking back, I've often wondered, was it my dream or was it my son's dream? Pam and I are like any other parents. If the kid wants to play piano, you get them piano lessons. They want to do this or that, you run with it. That's what we did, and I think that's how it always starts. But that isn't always where it ends. For too many kids, there comes a time when the kid loses the dream, and it becomes the parent taking over or pushing the dream further than where the kid wanted to go. Would my son have been happy playing Dixie Youth rec ball forever? I think not, but he enjoyed his friends.

What I mean to say is, perhaps he would have been just as happy if we hadn't spent so much time at the ballpark. We missed out going to the lake, fishing and camping, just going on vacations. Most of our vacation time was spent at the ballpark. Both Pam and I saved up vacation days to go to World Series events, and we'd fit in fun time around the ballpark. Now I look back on his family's busy life and wonder if things would have worked out differently if we hadn't thrown ourselves so fully into sport.

With this benefit of hindsight, I now feel I have the wisdom to advise other parents to sincerely question their motivation behind the constant push to promote their talented kids in sports, including whether participation in year-round traveling sports is the right idea for their family. While it's certainly healthy at some level to direct kids to not just thrive but succeed at their highest levels, it's also a slippery slope that may lead to unhealthy passions. These can undercut the well-being of a well-rounded family life. It can quickly and unknowingly cannibalize families' "down time" and break down important relationship connections. We missed out on the family time. We missed out on doing the things we liked together—like hunting and fishing— because we were at the ballpark, chasing this trophy or notoriety, when all that really mattered was being with my family. I see it now but didn't see it then.

We carved out one week per year for fun, when there was down time between major games. One week out of 52 weeks a year. We would head south, boat in tow, to the St. Jude Bass Classic fishing tournament on Sardis Lake, Mississippi. It was a way for us to do something other than baseball. While those times were—and are now—sacred to me, what other lost opportunities did we miss out on?

If I could impart one message to sporting families reading this book, it would be the importance of not having regrets concerning this lost time. I don't have any more moments. Those simple things he and I enjoyed, that we could have enjoyed but didn't because we were chasing something... what was it in the end? What does it get you? All those world series, all those national championships, what do they mean now? Trust me, in those ballparks, there's knockdown drag-outs chasing those things. I had a lot of significant memories with my son in the ballpark, but we sacrificed so much as a family—money-wise, time together. We were finally getting to that point with my son; it wasn't always just baseball.

Pam and I have a different mindset regarding raising Shelby with a healthy balance of life and sports. There's no pressure on Shelby when it comes to playing summer ball or competitive ball. I believe Shelby will get as much attention for her softball as her brother, given her natural talent, by playing at a measured pace and in her high school program.

Looking back, I think Stevo could have succeeded just as much as he did while only playing half of what he did because of his heart and skill set. I understand you've got to sacrifice some if you want to chase your dream. But are you sacrificing your family? Are you sacrificing your kids? To what extent are you sacrificing, and what is your real outcome? And while about 80 percent of the boys and maybe 80 percent of the girls I coached went on to play college ball, a lot of them aren't even playing anymore. I look at the teams we played against, whose kids and families were sacrificing like we were, and so many of them aren't playing anymore. So again, what's your real outcome for all the sacrifice?

Something I tend to look at when I think about this is the number of players we had move on to higher levels between the boys and the girls with our new tempered approach. On the boys' side, 22 of our players signed on to play college baseball, and the few that didn't were offered opportunities.

It was a remarkable accomplishment and gratifying that a few of those players are MLB draft prospects today. After we lost Stevo, we took a different approach with the girls, making sure we took more time off for families. Rather than seeing a reduction, we have 14 or more girls playing college softball now who filtered through our programs, and two of our younger group have already signed as well. There are many more in the works I'm sure, since these girls are still just sophomores and juniors in high school. Between our boys and girls teams, we've gone to two national championships, 10 world series championships, and numerous tournament championships. Athletic families tend to fear they will be harming their child's chances if they don't take advantage of every opportunity to play that comes, but in reality, you could be sacrificing your family's closeness as an unintended consequence.

As the sports seasons are so well organized and scheduled, it's easy to mark out on a calendar times when family vacation is on the docket. It is possible to balance the calendar—a family must be intentional. Carve out the real family vacation time by marking it down on a calendar that includes everything else. Try to get a solid number of days (more than a week if possible) each year just for family time. That's where the focus should be and allow the sports to come second. It's easy to tell yourself that you'll prioritize family time 'someday,' but that day never arrives, or it's too late when it does. Instead, sporting families should understand that what's important is to create the sporting life around the family schedule rather than the other way around.

As for my family, the scar, the disjointing of Stevo's passing, remains. Even after the acute numbness wore off, the family continues to feel dissipated. That void will always be there. Yet the enormous value and contribution that Stevo's 20 years on Earth have left to those who knew him also remain. While Pam and Shelby got tattoos of SK11 in his memory, I got my first full sleeve tattoo commemorating our hunting, fishing, and baseball together. These give us the opportunity to continue telling Stevo's story to those who never met him.

Grief never ends, but it changes. It's a passage, not a place to stay. While the pain never heals, you learn to cope. I remember seeing the grief come into my grandfather's eyes when, at age 78, he lost my uncle of almost 50 years old. That same grief came into my father's eyes when we lost my infant brother, Stephen, just a few days after he was born. It doesn't matter how old you are or how old the child at the point of losing them. Grief is not a sign of weakness, nor a lack of faith. It is the price of love.

THE END

If you'd like to make a contribution to the SK11 Training Facility or the Gamechanger Award, please contact:

Gamechangersk11@yahoo.com

ACKNOWLEDGMENTS

From our family to yours, we'd like to thank the following for your love and support through our journey:

Millington First Baptist Church

Andrew & Jordan Harbor Youth Minister

Jack and Brooke Suggs

Dianne & Bob Baker

Kingdom Men group - Millington First Baptist

Bart Garey

Howard Fuller

Clayton Allen

Tobey Anderson

FedEx

Air National Guard

Jonathan Day

Our Friends and Family

And You! Thank you for sharing our story.

CPSIA information can be obtained
at www.ICGtesting.com
Printed in the USA
LVHW091331100921
697437LV00012B/877